HOMEGROWN
Vegetables,
Fruits, and Herbs
A BOUNTIFUL, HEALTHFUL GARDEN FOR LEAN TIMES

CREATIVE
HOMEOWNER®

HOMEGROWN
Vegetables,
Fruits, and Herbs
A BOUNTIFUL, HEALTHFUL GARDEN FOR LEAN TIMES

Jim Wilson
Photography by Walter Chandoha

CREATIVE HOMEOWNER®, Upper Saddle River, New Jersey

HOMEGROWN VEGETABLES, FRUITS, AND HERBS

AUTHOR	Jim Wilson
PHOTOGRAPHER	Walter Chandoha
MANAGING EDITOR	Fran Donegan
EDITOR	Lisa Kahn
GRAPHIC DESIGNER	Kathryn Wityk
PHOTO COORDINATOR	Mary Dolan
PROOFREADER	Sara M. Markowitz
DIGITAL IMAGING SPECIALIST	Frank Dyer
INDEXER	Schroeder Indexing Services
COVER DESIGN	David Geer, Kathryn Wityk

CREATIVE HOMEOWNER

VICE PRESIDENT AND PUBLISHER	Timothy O. Bakke
ART DIRECTOR	David Geer
MANAGING EDITOR	Fran J. Donegan
PRODUCTION COORDINATOR	Sara M. Markowitz

Current Printing (last digit)
10 9 8 7 6 5 4 3 2 1

Manufactured in the United States of America

Homegrown Vegetables, Fruits, and Herbs
Library of Congress Control Number: 2009924287
ISBN-10: 1-58011-471-7
ISBN-13: 978-1-58011-471-4

CREATIVE HOMEOWNER®
A Division of Federal Marketing Corp.
24 Park Way
Upper Saddle River, NJ 07458
www.creativehomeowner.com

Planet Friendly Publishing
✓ Made in the United States
✓ Printed on Recycled Paper
 Text: 10%   Cover: 10%
Learn more: www.greenedition.org

GREEN EDITION

At Creative Homeowner we're committed to producing books in an earth-friendly manner and to helping our customers make greener choices.

Manufacturing books in the United States ensures compliance with strict environmental laws and eliminates the need for international freight shipping, a major contributor to global air pollution.

And printing on recycled paper helps minimize our consumption of trees, water, and fossil fuels. *Homegrown Vegetables, Fruits, and Herbs* was printed on paper made with 10% post-consumer waste. According to the Environmental Defense Fund Paper Calculator, by using this innovative paper instead of conventional papers we achieved the following environmental benefits:

Trees Saved: 27

Water Saved: 12,265 gallons

Solid Waste Eliminated: 745 pounds

Greenhouse Gas Emissions Eliminated: 2,547 pounds

For more information on our environmental practices, please visit us online at www.creativehomeowner.com/green

Dedication

This book is dedicated to the certified Master Gardeners of the USA and Canada, and especially to my Missouri Master Gardener, Janie Mandel, who has kept me from being overwhelmed by digital technology. —*J.W.*

Acknowledgments

Much of the material on these pages began as a syllabus I wrote for a course on Advanced Master Gardening and as a manual for coordinators of community gardens. During the process of turning it into this book, I learned as much as I contributed. I want to thank the editors and graphics specialists at Creative Homeowner for their masterly pruning of wordy passages and their elegant application of Walter Chandoha's images. —*J.W.*

Health & Safety First

ALL PROJECTS AND PROCEDURES in this book have been reviewed for safety; still it is not possible to overstate the importance of working carefully. What follows are reminders for plant care and project safety. Always use common sense.

■ Always consider nontoxic and least toxic methods of addressing unwanted plants, plant pests, and plant diseases before resorting to toxic methods. Follow package application and safety instructions carefully.

■ Always substitute rock phosphate and gypsum for bonemeal when amending soil. Authorities suggest that there's a hazard in using bovine-based products such as bonemeal, blood meal, and cow manure because they could harbor the virus that causes mad cow disease in cattle and humans.

■ Always read labels on chemicals, solvents, and other products; provide ventilation; heed warnings.

■ Always wear eye protection when using chemicals, sawing wood, pruning trees and shrubs, using power tools, and striking metal onto metal or concrete.

■ Always wear a hard hat when working in situations with potential for injury from falling tree limbs.

■ Always wear appropriate gloves in situations in which your hands could be injured by rough surfaces, sharp edges, thorns, or poisonous plants.

■ Always wear a disposable face mask or a special filtering respirator when creating sawdust or working with gardening dusts and powders.

■ Always protect yourself against ticks, which can carry Lyme disease. Wear light-colored, long-sleeved shirts and pants. Inspect yourself for ticks after gardening.

■ Always determine locations of underground utility lines before you dig, and avoid them by a safe distance. Buried lines may be for gas, electricity, communications, or water. Contact local utility companies, which will help you map their lines.

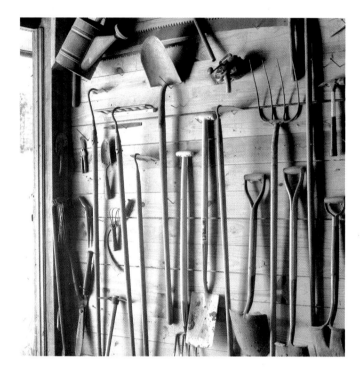

■ Always read and heed tool manufacturer instructions.

■ Always ensure that the electrical setup is safe; be sure that no circuit is overloaded and that all power tools and electrical outlets are properly grounded and protected by a ground-fault circuit interrupter (GFCI). Do not use power tools in wet locations.

■ Always keep your hands and other body parts away from the business ends of blades, cutters, and bits.

■ Never use herbicides, pesticides, or toxic chemicals unless you have determined with certainty that they were developed for the specific problem you hope to remedy.

■ Never allow bystanders to approach work areas where they might by injured by workers or work-site hazards.

■ Never work with power tools when you are tired or under the influence of alcohol or drugs.

■ Never carry sharp or pointed tools, such as knives or saws, in your pocket.

Foreward

Fat August is the season of plenty. Braids of onions hang to dry in the attic, pickles swim in tubs of brine, jars of canned tomatoes cool by the stove. There is joy in this abundance, joy in the faces of friends who crowd around our kitchen table for dinner, joy in watching them empty one platter after another.

We make no claim to total self-sufficiency. We are no strangers to the supermarket. We have jobs and medical coverage, the burdens and benefits of modern life. But every year we plant a vegetable garden, and we are the better for it.

It's more than economics. Yes, we usually end up with more homegrown food than we can consume on our own, though there are fewer calories in daikon than in doughnuts. And there are the grocery dollars saved.

Only a couple of us will ever become real farmers. But to raise something edible from seed is to bring forth sustenance from the earth. Raise your own sweet corn or a few potatoes, and you get a sense of where food comes from, a fresh respect for those who feed us. Serve those same vegetables, and you will be eating well indeed, for greatness in the kitchen begins in the garden.

While you will not be able to grow everything yourself, you will learn to appreciate farmers' markets and other local sources. You will find yourself seeking and celebrating the new, the unfamiliar, the delicious. For from a few small seeds, champion vegetables and vegetable champions are born.

Roger B. Swain
Host, PBS-TV's "The Victory Garden"

Contents

Introduction

Back in 2007, few Americans could have been persuaded to plant a food garden or to enlarge an existing vegetable patch. Then the economy began to unravel. Today, many families are looking for ways to reduce costs and to eat healthier, fresher, better-tasting food.

Food gardens, which for several decades took a backseat to ornamental landscapes, have begun to sound like a good idea to many folks with a sunny yard. This resurgence of interest in—and need for—homegrown food was what convinced my friend and colleague Walter Chandoha and me to come out of blissful retirement to create this book. Our goal is to help aspiring gardeners avoid the disappointment or downright failure that often comes with the first attempts at cultivating produce. We also hope to convince families who are already growing food crops to grow more, both for themselves and for the needy in their communities.

Through the advice and recommendations offered in *Homegrown Vegetables, Fruits, and Herbs*, we aim to hold the hand of the new gardener through that first year, when the learning curve is so steep that a novice can feel overwhelmed. Both Walter and I have mentored many a young gardener and have designed this book to be our surrogate. Most of all, we want to assure families that when the going gets tough, a big food garden can be like a friend indeed. It won't attempt to entertain you, but it will enlighten you and—eventually—repay all the time and attention you have invested in it with a bounty of delicious gifts.

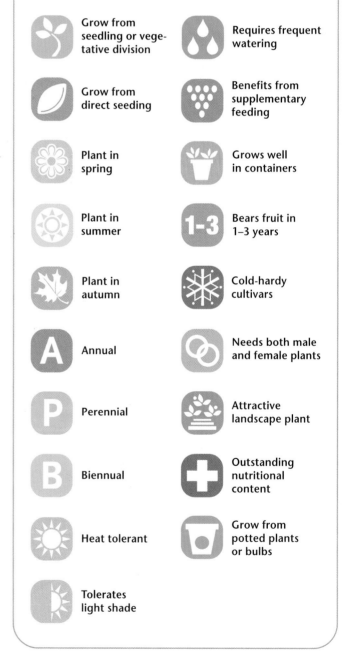

KEY TO Essential Stats

THE ICONS SHOWN BELOW were designed to assist readers in understanding basic planting, growing, and harvesting information for the vegetables, fruits, and herbs listed in Chapters 6–8.

Grow from seedling or vegetative division

Requires frequent watering

Grow from direct seeding

Benefits from supplementary feeding

Plant in spring

Grows well in containers

Plant in summer

1-3 Bears fruit in 1–3 years

Plant in autumn

Cold-hardy cultivars

A Annual

Needs both male and female plants

P Perennial

Attractive landscape plant

B Biennial

Outstanding nutritional content

Heat tolerant

Grow from potted plants or bulbs

Tolerates light shade

Ripe gooseberries gleam like jewels in the afternoon sun, top. Golden and ruby beets are just two of the varieties now available to home gardeners, below. Kikuza pumpkins, a rare Japanese heirloom variety, have orange flesh and a sweet yet spicy flavor, right.

Why Grow Your Own?

Even though I am bearded and wear socks with my sandals, I would make a poor prophet. Nevertheless, I see signs and portents that the lavish lifestyles and unrestrained spending that many once enjoyed are probably a thing of the past. Even when we get to the other side of this current economic crisis, most of us will think twice before buying goods and services we may want but don't actually need.

The Great Depression had a similar effect on my co-author, Walter Chandoha, and me. During those lean years, both our families worked hard to provide life's necessities, and that included growing and selling produce of all sorts. Unlike many who were less fortunate, we always had enough to eat year-round, thanks to home-canned fruits and vegetables and cured meats for winter meals. (Home freezers didn't exist in those days.)

You are probably reading this book because you're interested in starting a vegetable garden of your own but don't know where or how to begin. It's a paradox that in today's Internet Age, when information about nearly everything is easily available, many adults lack the most basic knowledge about growing food. We aim to change that.

On the pages that follow, you will find practical advice based on many decades of hands-on experience. We'll give you our tips on preparing your soil, the ideal times to plant in your area, fertilizing, weeding, mulching, nonhazardous pest and disease control, and much more. And in Chapters 6 through 8, you'll find photographs and detailed descriptions for planting, maintaining, and harvesting the most common vegetables, fruits, and herbs for maximum yield and enjoyment.

What is Responsible Gardening?

Throughout this book, you will learn how to grow wholesome, cost-effective food by practicing responsible gardening. By that, we mean using mostly organic fertilizers and following integrated pest management protocols. These involve using pest controls and herbicides that, when used as directed, are nontoxic to humans and do not accumulate in the soil. Some of the pest controls we use would not pass strict "organic" standards, but neither of us has the slightest qualms about eating food from plants sprayed with them. So there you have it, full disclosure. The vast majority of American gardeners follow similar food gardening practices, so we are in good company.

Neat rows of salad greens are as pleasing to the eye as they are to the palate.

Our methods might turn off a few "wannabe" food gardeners caught up in the current infatuation with all things organic. We don't ask that you agree with what we plant, how we fertilize our food crops, or how we minimize insect and disease damage. We do ask that you give proper weight to our hard-won experience in food gardening, well over 100 years between the two of us. We, too, appreciate the

value of gardening practices and products that have little or no negative environmental impact. But we know that many "organic" recommendations are made primarily for profit, or are based on anecdotal information without scientific research. We also know that many so-called organic pest controls are too expensive for the home gardener. We'll discuss the latest and best options available in soil amendments, mulches, fertilizers, and pest and disease control throughout the chapters of this book.

Cute, but not garden-friendly.

SMART *Gardener*

If you are new at growing food crops, start small. You will want a garden that is enjoyable as well as productive. Enlarge your garden as you begin to master the basics of soil and crop management. If weeds continue to best you, cut back on size.

ANYONE WHO HAS BEEN GROWING VEGETABLES and small fruit for a number of years can vouch for **the deep sense of satisfaction that comes with harvesting and preparing fresh produce from one's own garden.** There is an elemental, almost visceral feeling of "providing" that probably goes back to instincts developed during our hunter-gatherer days.

Those of us who lived through the Great Depression remember that back then, people felt obliged to garden. Even if they had enough money to buy fresh vegetables and fruit, it didn't feel right to have a good plot of land available and not use it productively. We were still close to the earth.

Many garden book authors write about the joy of gardening. However, there is a great difference between creating a beautiful landscape and the satisfaction you get from providing food for your family. Both flowers and food can bring joy to your life. Still, nothing can match the fulfillment that comes from keeping every square foot of your food garden in production all season long. Or the triumphant feeling when, just after harvesting a huge crop of vegetables and fruit, **you visit a supermarket and see what you would have paid for the same amount of produce.** Or the humility that will touch you when, just after you have delivered a load of homegrown vegetables to a food pantry, you see a parent taking home some of the vegetables you grew.

Protecting your health. Then there are health concerns to consider. Who knows when the next food recall will occur? Hardly any species of food crop has escaped contamination: tomatoes, spinach, jalapeno peppers, strawberries, melons, and so on. Of course, unless you have a big garden plot and live in a sunny climate, there is no way that you can get by without purchasing some fresh produce, especially during the winter months. So, "you pays your money and you takes your chances," and hope that your family will be spared from contaminated food. You also make a resolution to **buy shipped-in fresh produce only when you can't grow it or buy it locally.**

It would be very difficult to approach the nearly self-sufficient lifestyles we knew when we were children. City ordinances may forbid you to raise chickens or rabbits for food, and certainly not a pig, goat, or a milk cow. Some neighborhoods are so restricted by covenants that you may have to seek approval just to start a food garden.

When all is said and done, much will be up to you. Unlike me in my youth, you probably won't have a network of relatives living on farms to counsel you on what to grow and when to plant it. And they certainly won't be around to plow your garden plot. **But you have access to sources of information that didn't exist back then: the Extension Service, the Internet, and vastly improved seed and fruit tree catalogs.** You have every reason to expect success with your first food garden or in expanding an existing garden to include small fruits and tree fruits. If you are among the fortunate families who lost neither jobs nor a home during these lean times, share your good fortune by planting a garden big enough to produce lots of fresh produce for your local food pantry.

Cukes grow best vertically.

Just a little elbow grease.

Getting Started

Spiritual satisfaction is important, but so is the satisfaction you enjoy from managing a high-performance food garden. Here are a few practices that Walter and I have used with great success over the years:

Soil Tests

Attempting to grow crops without reliable soil testing is like setting out on a long, involved trip without a road map or a GPS device. The Web site of your state's Extension Service should give you directions for taking and sending in soil samples. Get an early start on sending your samples so that the standard two- to three-week processing time doesn't delay your planting. Then, submit soil samples every three or four years thereafter. These periodic soil tests will guide you in replacing plant nutrients in the soil that are removed every time you harvest a crop of vegetables. Composting every scrap of garden waste helps, but that cannot keep your soil's "bank account" of nutrients in balance. In all but a few inherently fertile soils, supplementary plant nutrients (fertilizers) will be needed.

SMART *Gardener*

Have your soil tested by your state's Extension Service. The major nutrients in most garden soils are deficient or out of balance, thanks to farming in years past and to heedless inversion of subsoil by contractors.

MULCHES *and* SOIL AMENDMENTS

THE MAJORITY OF GARDEN SOILS are composed partly or wholly of clay. These heavy soils need to be modified with large amounts of organic soil conditioners to make them workable. Such major soil modification is expensive, but you will pat yourself on the back after just one season of satisfying gardening with soil that is responsive to plant nutrients and open to absorbing water from sprinklers or soaker hoses.

All fertilizers work best in the presence of adequate organic matter in the soil, and compost, mulches, and soil amendments are among the best sources. As organic matter breaks down, it nourishes the beneficial soil organisms that help make nutrients accessible to plant rootlets. Soil conditioners mixed into the soil to spade depth are the major source of organic matter, but mulches applied on top of the soil also contribute a significant amount, mostly through the action of earthworms that tunnel up to the mulch/soil interface, ingest small particles of organic matter, and take them down into lower layers of soil. Earthworms leave a trail of "castings" as they tunnel—nutritious material that they ingest and expel in a form that can easily be taken up by plant root hairs. In Chapter 3, "Understanding Your Soil," beginning on page 38, we'll provide an in-depth discussion of soil types, amendments, conditioners, and fertilizers.

Keep weeds away from delicate spring lettuces by using generous amounts of straw mulch.

Irrigation

Many parts of the country are coping with restrictions on when and where water can be used in landscapes, and how much, if any, can be applied. No one could fault you if you choose to leave your lawn to nature's whims, and apply the saved water to your food garden. My family endured a long drought in California during the early 1970s. We were down to catching gray water from our washing machine and pouring it around shrubs and food plants to keep them alive.

You can economize on water use for food crops by running soaker hoses down rows. The slow drip of water from the porous rubber hoses minimizes evaporation by placing it in the root zone of plants rather than spraying it into the air. Sprinkler irrigation can evaporate or be blown away from your targeted plants. Even if you are not under restrictions on watering, you should consider drip irrigation to save money and ensure optimum growth of your plants. Drip irrigation does have a shortcoming, however; the water spreads horizontally only about nine inches to either side of the leaky hose or drip emitter. The cone of moist soil widens somewhat as the water gravitates down, but you still need to direct-seed or transplant seedlings close enough to the water source to meet the needs of plants for soil moisture.

Save water by switching from a sprinkler to soaker hoses.

KID-FRIENDLY VEGGIE RECIPE

BECAUSE SUMMER SQUASH—zucchini, yellow crookneck, and patty pan—is such a prolific producer, we ate a lot of it in our house—"we" meaning my wife, Maria, and I. Our six kids hated it. We could barely get them to eat their "no thank you" portion—a mouthful or two that was a mandatory policy at our dinner table. Even if they didn't like something, they had to at least try it, whatever it was.

As much as they disliked squash, they loved pizza. What's the most fragrant part of pizza? Oregano and garlic, and—if it's made my way—mozzarella and Parmesan cheese. So, I invented Pizza Squash. When they smelled pizza cooking, they were drawn to the kitchen. I told them I was cooking pizza made without dough. They tried it, liked it, and they still liked it, even after I confessed that it was a trick to get them to eat squash. — *Walter Chandoha*

Pizza Squash

Preheat oven to 400° F. Cut rounds of squash about ½-inch thick. (For larger portions slice the squash lengthwise.) Arrange slices on a cookie sheet; drizzle with olive oil. Turn each slice over so each side is oiled. Salt and pepper to taste. Bake 10-12 minutes until al dente. Remove from oven and top each round with shredded mozzarella, a pinch of grated Parmesan, a sprinkle of oregano, and a tiny bit of garlic powder. Return to oven set on broil until the cheese melts and turns a golden brown.

WEED *Control*

BACK WHEN I WORKED FOR A GARDEN SEED COMPANY, I was given the job of answering mail from home gardeners. There were often complaints about broadleaf weeds and grass seedlings that sprouted in rows planted with vegetable seeds. It was difficult to convince the letter writers that these weeds and grasses did not come from our vegetable seed packets, but from seeds that had been lying dormant in the soil for many years. Had I been able to talk to the gardener directly, I would have assured them that seed companies are fanatic about removing weed seeds during the milling and cleaning process.

Suffice it to say that you can expect "weedlings" to sprout from dormant seeds and roots that are present in the soil. **In a contest for soil moisture and plant nutrients, the weed seedlings will always win over the vegetable seedlings. You should be prepared to pull them out when they are small, or to dig out well rooted, older seedlings with minimum damage to nearby vegetable plants.** A dandelion digger is a great tool for digging out weeds, roots and all.

How does a beginner know a vegetable seedling from a "weedling"? It comes with observation and practice.

Only a few garden vegetable sprouts resemble grass. Onions and chives are good examples. So, as you study the row of emerging plants, good guys and bad guys, you can begin weeding by grasping the grass seedlings at ground level, pulling them out, and throwing them into the compost bin. Then, survey the remaining seedlings. If germination was strong, the good guys will outnumber the weeds. **One by one, pull out the seedlings that look different from the majority, or have a different foliage color or texture.** Weeding is a tedious process that can be physically and mentally tiring. But with the aid of a kneeling bench or pad and a music source plugged into your ear, you can switch off the urge to be somewhere else, doing something else. After one season of weeding, you'll remember the shape, color, and feel of vegetable seedlings you weeded. Not incidentally, **remember to take along your dandelion digger every time you kneel or sit down to weed.** If a weed seedling won't come out with a gentle tug, it may be the action end of a piece of perennial weed root or an acorn, hickory, or walnut seedling, all of which require undercutting and prying up before they'll come out, root and all.

Weeding in a fall garden.

Quick-growing lettuce is interplanted with longer-season cabbage (left). After harvesting cool-season vegetables, replant the bed with succession crops such as zucchini (below).

Interplanting

A few kinds of small, quick-growing vegetables are suitable for growing between larger, longer-season vegetables and small fruit. Foremost among these are leaf lettuce, mustard greens, onion sets, radish, spinach, and Swiss chard. A few kinds of annual herbs can also be wedged in between the hulking plants of large vegetables: cilantro, summer savory, parsley, and dwarf basils such as 'Spicy Globe' are good examples. Don't get carried away and try to interplant vegetables such as beans or cabbage. Their plants are vigorous enough to compete strongly with nearby large vegetables. Interplanting is a good use for excess seedlings you have pried out of rows of direct-seeded vegetables. Seedlings that are "pulled out by the ears" rather than dug out seldom survive transplanting.

Succession Planting

Here is where you will see good gardeners shine. They make it a personal challenge to be ready to pop in seeds or plants of a second or third crop as soon as they have harvested the first or second planting. They know that certain cool season vegetables need a month longer to mature than the speedy kinds, so they pay close attention to "days to maturity" for each kind they consider. In areas with a short growing season, they know to leave perhaps one-quarter of their garden open during spring because they realize that some spring crops might not mature quickly enough to allow timely planting of long-season, warmth-loving annuals.

The very best of the planners are like composers of music, but instead of hearing music in their heads, they see seasonal crops following seasonal crops, with none of the "dead air" silence so dreaded by radio and TV broadcasters. On page 22, you will find a few succession tips arranged by hardiness zones.

SMART *Gardener*

Site your garden where it will receive full sun all or most of the day, and where it will drain quickly after a rain without washing away. Place it well away from trees, keeping in mind that tree roots can spread well beyond the drip from the foliage canopy.

A labor of love... for beans!

THE FOLKS WHO WRITE THE DESCRIPTIVE COPY for seed packets and catalogs often use terms they assume everyone understands. Many beginning gardeners—and even some expert ones—would disagree. While many gardening words sound simple, you really do need to know the meaning behind them. So, stick with me while I give you a short course in "Seedspeak."

Vegetable nomenclature. Back in the eighteenth century, the Swedish botanist **Linnaeus first divided and subdivided the great kingdom of seed-bearing plants, using terms such as order, family, genus, and species.** Unfortunately, the seed trade relies on a different set of terms. For example, they use "kind" as a starting point. Beans, peas, and sweet corn are different "kinds" of vegetables. A kind is not the same as a genus or species. That is because so much crossing (both deliberate and accidental) has occurred that a kind might include genetic input from more than one genus or species.

Now, let's venture onto the slippery slope of varieties and hybrids. **Kinds are divided into varieties and hybrids.** When a seed breeder develops a new variety, it is named and photographed, and its characteristics are carefully documented. This visual and written information sets the standard for that variety from that point forward. **Seed people call this standard the "type" for the variety.**

The term "type" represents an average plant within a variety, and a certain amount of variation is to be expected. For example, if you planted a long row of seeds of, say, yellow wax beans and carefully examined each plant that grew from those seeds, you would notice a certain amount of difference in their size, pod length, and shape, and perhaps even a tendency for a few plants to form short runners.

Keeping that variation within a permissible range is a never-ending task for seed people. To do so, every few years the seed breeder is required to select a few very similar plants from a group of yellow wax beans. He or she plants these at a distance from any other varieties of beans. The seeds produced by these select yellow wax bean plants are then saved, and eventually become the new sales inventory for that variety. It can take as long as five years for enough seeds to be collected for this purpose, which is called "increasing."

Every generation of increase has to be monitored carefully, and "off-type" plants removed and composted. As a young seedsman, that was my job. I was sent out to seed fields where I ran a trained crew that walked down every row of beans or peas, looking for and pulling out any plant that was off-type. Usually, these were flat-podded beans mutating from a round-podded selection, or extremely robust plants that stood out among the uniform, smaller-size bush bean plants. Fields of peas grown for seed had to be monitored for pod shape and size, plant height, and freedom from a primitive mutant we called "rabbit-ear peas." The occasional rattlesnake slithering through the fields in search of rodents kept the job interesting.

Cross-Pollination. Of course, there was, and still is, some cross-pollination within the seed fields. You will see the term "open-pollinated" used frequently on seed packets and in catalogs. This means that every plant in the field is open for cross-pollination by pollen from surrounding plants. Even though beans tend to be self-pollinated, some crossing does happen, thanks to bees, flies, and wasps carrying pollen from one plant to another. Also, **a certain amount of genetic reversion to primitive plants takes place; this is why off-type plants have to be culled out.** The result of all this labor is that when you buy and plant a packet of round-podded, white-seeded, bush bean variety, that is what you should expect. The same applies for any other open-pollinated kind of vegetable.

Seed breeders are incurable optimists. They're forever convinced that any variety can be made even better by selecting and increasing superior plants. **Often, however, Mother Nature produces changes resulting in entirely new varieties—take eggplant, for example.** I remember when virtually all eggplant varieties took many weeks to set fruit, and the results were big, clunky, hard-shelled, egg-shaped, and full of seeds that tended to be bitter.

Then a breeder in New Hampshire found an extra-early-fruiting eggplant, increased its seeds, and introduced it to home and commercial growers, who up until then had been unable to grow eggplant successfully. Then, Japanese seed breeders found a plant that produced long, slender, tender-skinned eggplant fruit and introduced the variety 'Ichiban'. Later, **a European seed breeder deduced that the market was ready for a colorful, tender-skinned, pink-purple-white eggplant that would not fall apart when sliced and grilled. It is available as 'Italian Tricolor'.** Now, there might have been some hybridization during the breeding process, but once the new type was established, seeds were produced in open-pollinated fields. Isn't Mother Nature awesome!

Hybrids

The first commercially available, man-made hybrid vegetables were sweet-corn hybrids introduced during the 1920s. Since that time, many hybrids within several kinds of vegetables have been released. Ironically, these do not include beans or peas because trials have shown that **hybrid beans or peas show little superiority over open-pollinated varieties.** While plant breeders do introduce new genetic traits to beans or peas by cross-pollinating them, once the trait has been transferred and stabilized, they increase the seeds in open-pollinated fields.

Let's take hybrid tomatoes as an example. One of the best-known hybrids for many years was 'Big Boy'. Seed breeders developed and evaluated many "parent" lines. Some were found to be good at forming abundant crops of seeds and were designated "female" parents. Some produced pollen in abundance and were used as "male" parents. Each parent line was maintained by self-pollination, and each was called an "inbred."

When you cross a female inbred with a male inbred, you get fruits containing hybrid seeds. You also get more than a sum of the parts, because a genetic phenomenon called "hybrid vigor" kicks in and the plants grown from hybrid seeds are far more vigorous than their inbred parents. Plant breeders evaluated many, many experimental crosses before deciding to introduce 'Big Boy'. **(Notice the single quotation marks? That's how the given names of hybrids or varieties are supposed to be written.)**

I knew the breeder of 'Big Boy' but we never got around to discussing the parents used to make the hybrid. I can only speculate that one of the parents bore large, smooth, well-shaped, deep-red fruit, while the other contributed good flavor and resistance to several tomato diseases. Back then, the pollen from the female would be removed by hand, both to prevent self-pollination and to allow pollen from the male to be transferred to the female via a camels-hair brush.

Nowadays, some hybrid tomato seeds are produced by using a female that is self-sterile. In other words, it can't pollinate itself. It can be pollinated by pollen from a different inbred, however.

Whatever means of hybridizing is used, the plants grown from hybrid seeds closely resemble each other, unlike varieties grown from open-pollinated seeds. They also set and ripen fruits within a few days of each other. No doubt that hybrid seeds are more expensive, but they are worth it because of their increased production and resistance to diseases.

Kohlrabi is usually green, but this red variety adds color and crunch when chopped or grated in a salad.

Hardiness Zones 9–10*

In these areas, which include low elevation gardens in California, winters are comparatively warm and nearly frost-free, and spring seasons are short and often warm. Varieties considered "spring vegetables" elsewhere are planted during the fall season in these two zones. Broccoli, Brussels sprouts, cabbage, and cauliflower, all cool-season vegetables that take several weeks to mature, need to be planted in early fall in order to shape up before cold wet winter weather sets in. Warm-season vegetables need to be planted during the spring in order to be harvested before the onset of the intense heat of September and October.

The hot months of fall in these zones are great for maturing fruits of long-season melons and hard-shelled squash that were planted in early summer. The combination of intense heat and dryness during fall months interferes with pollination and can rule out late summer plantings of many kinds of vegetables.

Hardiness Zones 6–8*

The frost-free span in these zones ranges from six to eight months, so two or three succession crops are possible. Early spring plantings of leafy vegetables and onions are

It's possible to plant a second crop of sweet corn in Zone 8, after the first crop succumbs to heat and humidity.

followed by early summer plantings of warmth-loving beans, eggplant, peppers, okra, southern peas, sweet corn, sweet potatoes, and tomatoes. **A quick second crop of tomatoes and sweet corn is possible in Zone 8 when the first crop peters out because of heat and humidity.** The month of August is the traditional time for planting seeds of fall greens and root crops to follow heat-resistant summer annuals. Thinnings from the crop of greens can be taken during the fall, leaving the main crop to be harvested prior to the onset of very cold weather in January or February. Among the summer crops, okra and sweet potatoes occupy garden space for the longest time. In the Southeast, late crops of sweet corn are occasionally interplanted with pumpkins or the green-and-white striped winter squash called cushaw. These aren't harvested until around Halloween, too late to be followed with crops of greens or root crops.

Hardiness Zones 3–5*

Zone 3 gardeners, while blessed with relatively cool summers and long summer days, are severely restricted in what and when they can plant. Certain areas within the zone can be visited by light frosts during summer months. Succession planting usually means following a spring-planted crop of greens, root crops, or onion sets with a crop of fall greens direct-seeded in mid-July. **Gardeners in Zone 3 have to be ready with floating row covers to protect tender crops from occasional light summer frosts.** They make the most of their garden space by spring plantings of cole crops (broccoli, cabbage, cauliflower, kale, and kohlrabi), peas, and rutabaga. Their long summer days favor the development of very large plants despite the relatively cool air. Long-day onions and carrots are mainstay summer vegetables for them.

Gardeners have more leeway in Zones 4 and 5. **Their spring seasons are long and cool enough to produce excellent broccoli, cabbage, potatoes, peas, and onions from early spring plantings.** A few summer nights may drop into the 40s, but summer frosts are rare. Thus, the classic sequence of quick-maturing, cold-tolerant kinds planted in early spring, followed by warm-weather annuals is possible. Unfortunately, fall frosts can come in September or, at the latest, early October, which means that only the spring-planted kinds will be off the ground in time for direct-seeding fall crops of cold-hardy vegetables in late July or early August. It's prudent to reserve a row or two for timely planting of fall crops.
Please refer to hardiness zone maps on pages 180–181.

The Science of Gardening, Enhanced by Experience

I wish I had access to the abundance of gardening information on the Internet before I planted my first food garden. It is a marvelous tool, as are all the additional sources of information now available. But I planted my first garden in the late 1940s. At the time, most books on vegetable gardening seemed to be written by English majors who were more skilled at turning a phrase than in the practicalities of gardening. So, I gardened by trial and error, as did Walter, while he was mastering the art of garden photography.

The *science* of gardening is a different matter. Back then, gardening knowledge was mostly gained through hands-on experience rather than clinical research. Gradually—and still a work in progress—the growth and development processes of plants are becoming better understood. It was not until the advent of Master Gardening courses offered by the County Cooperative Extension Service at state universities that the science of gardening opened to the home gardener. I was privy to it earlier through my education in agronomy, but I am happy to listen and learn when in the presence of the new generation of soil and plant scientists.

A recycled stepladder is reincarnated as an herb garden.

SMART *Gardener*

The tomato thief. While I realize this story has little to do with getting your garden started, it is a precautionary tale you'll soon appreciate. I had been watching my hybrid 'Beef-eater' tomatoes like a hawk. One night, two fruits were only a day or so away from picking. The following morning, these big, once-lovely tomatoes had been twisted off and chewed, but not devoured. Now, a rabbit can't twist off a tomato, and there were no deer tracks. Both red and gray squirrels are daytime feeders. No other vegetables were eaten, so that ruled out the piggy groundhogs. That left raccoons. That night, I donned gloves, set up a humane trap, and baited it with aromatic, fully ripe cantaloupe. Unfortunately, it seems that I lost this particular raccoon con game. Recently, I turned on the exterior floodlights and saw three yearling coons clinging to my finch feeder, filching expensive seeds. Still, I'm thankful that armadillos have yet to find my garden. I'm grateful for small favors.

Where and How
Does Your
Garden Grow?

During World War II, many Americans planted Victory Gardens in side yards, front yards, vacant lots—in short, wherever there was sun and a bit of space. A typical urban lot in those days would have been 50 to 60 feet wide by 100 to 150 feet deep, and some were much smaller. There were few suburbs back then.

Urban sprawl continued until the last stop of the trolley line, where it gave way to pastures and farms. Backyards were small, often shaded by trees, and usually used as play areas for kids and pets. The only truly spacious lots surrounded the elegant homes of wealthy families. Thus, front-yard food gardens were a common part of the streetscape, much like flowers and shrubs are today.

Many things have changed since those times, but the nuts and bolts of choosing a site for a productive food garden remain the same. In fact, you might find that the information in this

chapter points you toward creating a modern Victory Garden in your own front yard. Our advice for starting and maintaining a small garden is applicable no matter where you live—in the city, the suburbs, or out in the country. We have also provided tips on growing fruit, many of which can be blended into a food garden without shading adjacent vegetables or creating root competition. Several species of small fruit will grow compatibly with vegetables. What's more, fruit is generally more expensive to buy, pound-for-pound, than vegetables.

Selecting a Site

To create a productive vegetable and fruit garden, you must begin with the fundamentals. The most important things you must consider include

Sunlight

Full sun is preferable, by far. No vegetables, fruits, or herbs will grow well in dense, daylong shade, and all but rhubarb will be challenged by light or mottled shade for most of the day. Most kinds will endure either afternoon or morning shade but will produce less than they would in full sun. (Before you gardeners in desert or semitropical areas raise your eyebrows, we acknowledge that afternoon shade can actually be beneficial where sunlight is extremely intense.) Midsummer—when the sun beams straight down at noon—is not the best time for evaluating how shadows might affect food production. Also keep in mind that shadows from trees and buildings cover more ground during spring and fall months, which are the most enjoyable seasons for working in a food garden.

Root Competition

Tree roots can reach out 1½ times as far as the diameter of the foliage canopy. Trees are like 800-pound gorillas; when they want water and nutrients, they will take them and will suck lesser plants dry while also robbing them of plant nutrients. Cutting invasive tree roots yearly with a spade won't work for long. Roots will retake the moist, porous soil of a food garden in a matter of weeks. Moral: site your garden well away from sizeable trees.

Drainage

You need to consider both surface and internal drainage. All vegetables and herbs grow best in moderately well-drained soil. Wet soil warms slowly in the spring and is more likely to harbor organisms that cause root rot. Loose, sandy soil drains too rapidly if not modified with organic matter.

Before you select a site for a food garden, traverse it like a golfer assessing the best track for a long putt. Look for a good, uniform slope that can carry away heavy rainfall. If the area is level, you will need to build up beds to give vegetables well-drained root runs. Make sure there are no low spots or swales where runoff from higher areas could create gullies or where water could stand for a day or two. Internal drainage is a function not only of soil type (clay, loam, silt, or sand), but also of how much you modify your soil with organic matter. (For more information about soil amendments, see Chapter 3, page 44.)

Water

The old prescription of "an inch of water per week" won't cut it for food gardens during hot, dry spells, and rarely do summer rains occur weekly. So, plan on irrigating every four to seven days, and providing at least an inch of water each time. That entails a lot of moving of water hoses, so you should site your garden as near as possible to a faucet. One faucet with a "Y" adapter can handle two hoses with sprayers, or soaker hoses laid down the center of raised beds.

Some homes are equipped with water softeners. Make sure that your outside faucets are not connected to the softener, or you may be irrigating your food and flower gardens with sodium-laced water. If water is scarce in your community, consider installing soaker hoses made of porous material down each row to provide drip irrigation. You might also install a catch-barrel for rainwater. Connect it to a downspout from your roof.

Frost Pockets

Certain areas around homes tend to trap cold air and cause plants to suffer frost damage. Fences or borders of evergreen shrubs can cause this, as can hills, slopes, or outbuildings that abut the low end of the area. Look for a site where air can move freely. Air flow is especially important for small fruit plants, which can be badly damaged by late frosts.

Property-line beet garden.

> **SMART** *Gardener*
>
> *If you use a sprinkler, you can measure its output by placing an empty can within the sprinkler pattern and recording how long it takes to collect an inch of water.*

Greens and onions grow in a raised bed right outside the kitchen.

DEALING WITH *Garden Critters*

DEER ARE NOT A PROBLEM in some suburban developments, but in other neighborhoods they can wreak havoc on the landscape. Even Bambi lovers can come to hate the destruction they cause. **Wild animals tend to follow parkland, creeks, and ravines into housing areas.** They tend to avoid yards where they have to cross streets or highways to gain access. Dogs can also be a deterrent, but not always.

Where deer are a problem, the right type of fence is the realistic solution. **A determined buck can clear a 6-foot fence easily, and with a running start, an 8-foot fence.** An effective barrier is a picket fence topped by tall pieces of electrical conduit strapped to posts, with taut wire running at 6- and 8-foot levels. Some gardeners prefer shorter posts with electrified wires at 6-, 12-, and 48-inch levels.

More anti-critter options. Eight-foot-high, plastic-net deer fences are cosmetically acceptable and do a good job of keeping deer out. Even when deer are not a problem, gardeners may still deal with rabbits, groundhogs, squirrels, and, in the South, armadillos. **Rabbits can be kept out of the garden with chicken-wire barriers,** but groundhogs and squirrels can climb and are best controlled by electrified fencing. Groundhogs are vigorous diggers, as are armadillos. You'll need to sink chicken-wire barriers at least a foot into the ground to discourage them. As a last resort, use a humane trap, and ask your wildlife agent where to relocate the trapped beasties.

A 5-foot-high picket fence around my food garden has kept deer out for several years. However, I also planted shrubs around the outside of the fence. Deer can't get close enough to see what is inside and, being cautious by nature, won't risk jumping. I stapled a hardware-cloth rabbit barrier around the base of the fence, and I am careful to keep the garden gates closed. **Farm supply stores are among the best sources of information on electrified fences to keep out deer.** You should be able to find one in an outlying town that serves farmers. Try the Internet and your State Extension Service.

Raspberries grow undisturbed inside this wood and chicken-wire "cage" (above). A half circle of wire fencing arched over a planting bed protects seedlings from greedy varmints (opposite, bottom).

A mild electric current deters deer from entering this garden.

SMART *Gardener*

Please don't whack yon serpent. *I welcome nonvenomous snakes to my garden because they keep rodents under control. Growing up on a farm in Mississippi, I learned the difference between pit vipers and harmless garter and rat snakes, and even the loudly hissing but innocuous hog-nose snake. I will pick up and move the harmless little ones so they don't frighten my garden partner, but I settle for using a hoe handle to guide big rat snakes out of high-traffic areas in our landscape and food garden. They can inflict a nasty bite, not venomous, but to be avoided. The larger nonvenomous snakes help keep voles, moles, and field mice under control, and the little guys eat insects.*

PREPARING YOUR *First Garden Plot*

HERE IS HOW TO GET YOUR SOIL READY for the first year of food gardening:

1. In early spring, take soil samples and send them to your state's Extension Service for testing. It should take several weeks to receive your results.

2. Buy a couple of bundles of 30-inch wooden surveyor's stakes and a large ball of sisal twine, at least 1,000 feet in length.

3. Buy at least a quart of organically approved, fatty-acid, top-kill herbicide. You may need two or three quarts, depending on the size of your plot and how coarsely you set the sprayer.

4. Purchase a couple of 2-gallon pump sprayers. Dedicate one to insecticides and the other to fatty-acid herbicides. Label the tanks in large letters using a felt-tip pen. Organic gardeners sometimes object to any form of spray or dust for insect, weed, or plant disease control, preferring to use biological controls. However, outbreaks of pests can spread while you are waiting for biological controls to take effect. **A safe and reasonable course of action is to use quick-acting controls that are nontoxic to humans.** Insecticidal soaps, Bt, and Neem oil for insects, and iron phosphate for slugs and pill bugs are typical of such controls.

A weedy patch of garden before work begins (top). The same patch after weeds are removed, soil is tilled, and compost is added (bottom).

5. Drive stakes at the ends of one side of the plot. Using a flexible measuring tape, position the remaining corner stakes before driving them in. The plot doesn't have to be perfectly square or rectangular, but it will look neater that way.

6. This next step is quite important: **wait until the air temperature is above 60° F and there is no wind.** Make up a solution of herbicide in one of the 2-gallon sprayers, and add a dash of dishpan detergent. Follow the directions for dilution; do not assume that if one tablespoonful of herbicide is good, two are better.

7. Lay a water hose across one end of the plot to mark off a 4-foot wide strip. Lay another hose parallel with the first and at a 4-foot distance away.

8. Spray the vegetation between the two hoses using the prepared solution, walking backwards slowly. Set the nozzle to a coarse spray; fine mists tend to drift onto desirable vegetation. Keep the nozzle close to the ground to minimize spray drift.

9. Move the first hose to mark off the next strip and spray it. Continue re-laying hoses and spraying until the entire plot has been sprayed. Wait at least a week before tilling the plot. Weeds should be dead or dying.

10. Rent a large tiller, around 8 hp or more. When the soil is moderately dry and crumbly, not sopping wet, till the plot. Pick up sticks and stones as you go.

11. Apply an organic fertilizer, such as Bradfield Organics, if soil tests indicate a deficiency of nitrogen, phosphate, or potash. Bagged chicken or sheep manure also work well, but be prepared for a ripe odor when it rains. **Add lime only if indicated by soil tests.** If you do apply lime, use a pelletized, dolomitic product.

12. Haul in and spread soil conditioner 3 inches deep. Till the soil again to mix in the fertilizer and organic soil conditioner.

13. Here's where the job becomes laborious: stretch a twine line tied to stakes down the long dimension of the plot, 6 feet in from the edge.

14. Create raised planting areas. Working your way down the line, shovel soil from beneath the line onto what will become your first raised planting row. Then, shovel soil from along the exterior border atop the bed. Your aim should be to excavate interior aisles about 30 inches wide and 6 inches deep, and to toss the excavated soil atop the raised bed. **You want the raised area to measure 4 feet wide at its crown.** Aisles need to be wide enough for passage by a wheelbarrow at the peak growth of the vegetable crop. Remove roots of perennial grasses and weeds as you go. Do not put them in your compost pile.

15. After roughly completing one bed, move the twine over and repeat the process to create another 4-foot-wide raised bed. While you are shoveling soil, someone else can be raking the raised beds level and removing clumps of vegetation, sticks, and stones.

16. Shovel out cross-aisles to shorten the distance necessary to walk around a row.

17. After completing and leveling the raised beds, spread mulch down the aisles. Bring in oscillating sprinklers for one hour.

18. Wait two weeks for newly exposed weed seeds to sprout, and spray again using herbicide. **Spray only when the air temperature is at 60° F or higher and the wind is still.**

19. Wait seven to ten days for the herbicide to work, then plant.

20. If deer have been seen in the neighborhood, you can assume they will destroy your garden. If your garden is not near children, a 5-foot-high electrified fence may provide adequate protection. Before adding one, check with the building department for requirements. There are fence kits available that provide a safe shock that is designed to deter pests.

21. Elsewhere, special plastic-net fencing designed to keep out deer will suffice. Galvanized electrical conduit in 10-foot lengths makes good posts. The posts will stand upright more easily if they are socketed into 2-foot lengths of PVC pipe sunk into holes driven into the ground.

22. **You can construct a simple gate by threading a conduit post through the end of the fencing and securing it in several places using water-resistant adhesive tape.** You can then use short lengths of elastic tie-downs to pull the end of the fence snug against the gatepost. Of course, remember to lock the gate when not in use. The gatepost may need to be braced, as will the corner posts.

Planting garlic seedlings.

A One-Time-Only Delay

At this point, you probably realize that spraying of herbicide will delay your planting. If you have also concluded that you will miss the planting window for early, cool-weather vegetables, you would also be right. But remember, this is a one-time-only delay. Treating with herbicide shouldn't be necessary in succeeding years.

However, if you insist on spring crops in the first year, start your soil preparation in late summer, before fall rains set in and complicate matters. Spraying needs to be completed before daytime air temperatures fall *below* 60° F. Don't rake the new raised beds smooth; leave them rough over the winter months to catch moisture and to reduce erosion.

The following spring, rake the beds just before planting time to kill the few surviving weed and grass seedlings. Before raking, shovel soil that has washed into aisles back atop the raised beds. Spread mulch in the aisles to allow all-weather access.

MY STAND ON *Organic Gardening*

MANY OF MY FRIENDS ARE TOTALLY COMMITTED to organic gardening. I respect their right to garden in any way they please, but ask that they spare me the evangelistic fervor. I am dedicated to raising the greatest amount of healthy food in the shortest amount of time, and at the lowest cost. If it means using conservative amounts of processed fertilizer and integrated pest management to reach that goal, I will do it, and I won't lose any sleep over not being 100 percent organic. **In the distant future, scientists might perfect benign ways to control garden pests and weeds at a modest cost, but we aren't there yet.**

Organic gardeners like to maintain that theirs is the "natural" way to garden. No garden is natural: all are imposed upon the landscape. **Our challenge is to manage our food gardens in such a way that little or no damage is done to the environment** and the produce will pass the highest safety and nutrition standards.

I have seen several gardens planted by organic gardeners who refused to use any herbicide. Every one of them suffered severe weed problems for two or three years, until thorough and timely pulling of weed and grass seedlings reduced the population. True, a few determined weeds will survive two sprayings with top-kill herbicide, but nothing like the overwhelming number that will survive tilling and no treatment with herbicide.

In this community garden, fresh, nutritious food for many families is grown using primarily organic methods.

What to Grow and How Much

Think like the manager of a small business when planning a food garden. Will you get back in value as much as you invest in time and effort? Probably not, if your garden is less than 500 square feet, or 20 x 25 feet in size. (Try picturing two small bedrooms side by side for a better idea of these dimensions.) This is not to say that small gardens are not worth your time and effort. They deliver many emotional and physical benefits, in addition to truly fresh and flavorful vegetables. Perhaps just as important is that a small garden is easier to manage.

How much can you consume? When you step up the size of your vegetable patch—to 1,000 square feet or larger—you can begin to quantify true cost savings. It is then possible to grow many kinds of vegetables for less than you would pay per pound at the supermarket. Make no mistake, though: when you plant a large food garden, you become a farmer, and farming of vegetables means work, some of it during weather that drives wimpy souls indoors to the comfort of air-conditioning.

How much of a given crop you should plant depends upon how and when it will be consumed. Will the vegetables go straight from the garden to your table, or do you plan to freeze or preserve some of your bounty for later use? With a number of types, such as tomatoes, zucchini, and cabbage, you can do both. But other crops, such as lettuce and radishes, can only be eaten fresh. When planting those vegetables, think of the old hair cream slogan: "A little dab will do ya." You also have to consider whether you will be vacationing during summer harvest season. What a waste if your tomato, corn, and pepper yields ripen for picking when you are away!

Because the number of feet of row you'll need to plant is best learned

Harvesting escarole.

from experience, count on your first year or two of gardening to produce "feast or famine" results. You can help matters by reviewing vegetable garden plans on the Internet. (The Hume Seeds Web site is a good source.) Many such sites offer guidelines on how much of each kind of vegetable to grow for a family of four. This will give you a good starting point.

Average Days to Maturity

Choose efficient kinds to get the biggest bang for your buck. "Efficient" vegetables are those that produce the maximum amount of food within a given area and time. "Average days to maturity" is listed on all seed packets and is included in the description of each variety in seed catalogs. This gives you a rough estimate of the days required for a crop to mature from direct-seeding (planting seeds straight from the packet) into garden rows or beds. Average days to maturity can range from 27 days for early-maturing radish varieties to 110 days for certain hard-shelled squash. When you set out (transplant) seedlings rather than seed, you cut an average of eight weeks off the posted maturity date. If you garden in hardiness zone 3, 4, or 5, you have a relatively short frost-free growing season. Because of this, the average days-to-maturity information is a critical factor in choosing varieties for your garden.

Whether it's the fruit of a plant or the plant itself that's eaten is another factor in its efficiency, as are the number of pickings you can make. Tomatoes, peppers, okra, eggplant, and ever-bearing strawberries are among the most efficient crops because you can pick their fruit over an extended period. Cabbage, collards, kale, and Swiss chard are efficient because you can either eat the entire plant or harvest bottom leaves and stems as they mature. Sweet corn is not efficient. Once you have pulled an ear or two from a stalk, that's it. However, I believe that the flavor of fresh-picked corn makes up for its inefficiency.

Containers can double your growing space.

Growing from Seeds and Seedlings

When I was fresh out of "cow college," I worked for a garden-seed company. During the early 1900s, that company retained famous artists to create posters for display in feed and seed stores. One of their most popular images was of a small girl holding a potted plant aloft and exclaiming, "My seed's up!" Adults also experience much the same thrill when they see a good stand of seedlings emerging from the soil. After all these years, I sure do. However, I realize that these baby plants depend on me for protection, so I promptly snap out of my reverie and scatter bran bait mixed with iron phosphate to control slugs, snails, earwigs, and pill bugs.

SMART *Gardener*

Learn how to balance rapidly growing plants with slower-growing varieties so that you can keep your garden producing food at a steady pace throughout the growing season. You can practice with direct-seeding plants that germinate and grow rapidly, but also buy plant kinds that grow slowly and take two or three weeks for seeds to germinate. You'll find detailed information on kinds of vegetables and how to grow them in Chapter 6, beginning on page 86.

Cool-Season Crops from Seeds

Experienced gardeners shake their heads in disbelief when they see people buying plants of cool-season kinds that would grow just as well or better from direct-seeding (sowing seeds in the garden). Many of these crops are needed in such quantities that starting from plants is unnecessarily expensive. Among the cool-season crops that are best started by direct-seeding in early spring are beets, chard, cilantro, kohlrabi, lettuce, mustard greens, green peas, radishes, spinach, and snap peas. (The reason I specify green peas is that southerners also plant warm-season "southern peas," including blackeye, crowder, and purple hull.)

Direct-seeding of cool-season crops past a short window of time in the spring is virtually useless. Hot weather and long days will cause cool-season crops to either shoot up heads of flowers and go to seed or become too bitter to eat. This is why experienced gardeners prepare garden beds in the fall. They only have to rake them lightly to get them ready for spring seeding. Over much of the country, late summer is the preferred time to direct-seed second plantings of greens and root crops. Endive and escarole grow especially well when fall-planted, as do the southern staples collard greens and turnips.

Quick-growing radishes are cool-season crops that are best started by direct-seeding.

A HEAD OF ROMAINE, iceberg, or other loose-leaf lettuce sells for about two dollars in most markets. You can buy a packet containing more than 100 lettuce seeds for about the same price.

Curious about how much a packet of seed would produce, **I scattered a couple of generous pinches of lettuce seed atop some seed-starting potting soil in two 6-inch flowerpots.** Some weeks later the sprouted seedlings were transplanted into plastic cell packs—one seedling per compartment. There were so many seedlings that I stopped transplanting when I ran out of empty cell packs.

I grew enough lettuce from that little experiment to feed my family green salads from early spring until the onset of summer. I gave lots of starts to my gardening friends and enough mature lettuce to supply the local food pantry at regular intervals. And there was enough seed left in that starter packet to grow plants for fall and early winter salads. In fact, I got so much lettuce that I wondered why it was so expensive at the supermarket.

Other vegetables are equally economical. Most seed packets contain more seed than should be planted at one time. **Stagger plantings, some today and then another in three or four weeks.** By spacing plantings weeks apart you'll avoid the feast or famine phenomenon. Even the seeds in a packet of expensive heirloom tomatoes will make more plants than can fit in most gardens. Seeds are a big bargain if planted frugally. Leftover seed? Put them in empty prescription pill bottles and store in the fridge. — *Walter Chandoha*

Cool-Season Crops from Seedlings

The cool-season kinds that are customarily set out as seedlings in the spring and again in late summer are broccoli, cabbage, and cauliflower. Cool-season crops transplanted in very early spring need protection from hard frosts. Experienced gardeners know to shelter their plants using plastic milk jugs with their bottoms cut off and their caps removed, or with spun-bonded acrylic floating row covers.

In the Deep South and low elevations of the West, gardens pass quickly from winter to summer with virtually no cool spring weather. In these zones, cool-season crops are best planted during late summer or early fall, in time for them to come to near-maturity before the onset of short, wet, winter days.

In recent years, shipping costs have raised the price of potatoes so drastically that it has become more cost-effective to grow them in home gardens. Potatoes, called "Irish potatoes" in some parts of the South, are a cool-season crop, and are usually started in early spring from "seed pieces." These are cut from whole, disease-free "seed potatoes" purchased at garden centers or ordered by mail.

When you divide a seed potato into pieces, each piece should have an "eye," which is a juvenile sprout. Dusting the freshly cut seed piece with powdered sulfur—which you can purchase in small bags at your local garden center—helps prevent the pieces from rotting before the sprouts emerge from the ground.

Special seed potatoes are readied for planting.

Direct-seeding of Frost-Tender Crops

You will get better results by direct-seeding the following frost-tender crops: beans, cantaloupes, cucumbers, honeydew and Crenshaw melons, okra, squash, southern peas, sweet corn, and watermelons. Seeds of these vegetables should be sown one to three weeks after the frost-free date for your area. They mature from midsummer on. Carefully observe the "distances apart" instructions on the seed packet, and thin plants accordingly. Too-close spacing will stunt plants.

The warm-season, frost-tender kinds that are customarily planted as seedlings soon after the average frost-free date are eggplant, peppers, sweet potatoes, and tomatoes. Sweet potato seedlings, commonly called "slips," are produced from sprouting roots. The sprouts draw on the nutrients stored in the fleshy root to form fibrous root systems and are sold by the bunch as well as in individual pots. Ornamental sweet potatoes—the ones with purple, chartreuse, or varicolored foliage—can form large roots, but they are not of eating quality.

MORE TIPS ON *Efficient Vegetable Growing*

Many kinds of vegetables are considered efficient because they occupy the soil for only a short period of time. Most of these are planted early in the spring (fall where winters are mild) and mature within a span of two months. Chinese cabbage, lettuce, mustard greens, peas, bunching onions, radish, and spinach are usually direct-seeded. A second crop of these cool-loving vegetables (except for peas) can be planted in mid-to-late summer for fall maturity.

Gardeners in the Deep South typically wait until around August 15 before planting turnips, mustard, spinach, and collard greens. There, these frost-hardy, highly nutritious crops mature quickly and yield a lot of food for the space occupied. In the Deep South and warm Southwest, green peas and snap peas can be planted in late summer for fall and winter harvesting. Elsewhere, fall frosts kill pea vines before they can mature pods.

Plant compact varieties of vining, spreading vegetables

Some kinds of vegetables spread so widely that they take up a lot of space and thus are not appropriate for small gardens. However, you can buy "compact" varieties of most vining vegetables. Whereas standard varieties of **pumpkins, hard-shelled winter-keeper squash, cantaloupes, watermelons, cucumbers, and sweet potatoes can form runners 8 to 12 feet in length,** compact varieties of these crops spread, on average, only half as far.

Like potatoes, the price of onions has risen at the market. Fortunately, this heavy-yielding crop has become one of the most efficient you can grow. Onions are cool-season crops, planted in early spring over most of the country, late summer in the Deep South. Really big, sweet, slicing onions are grown from seedlings. Onion sets, on the other hand, are small bulbs produced from seeds that are genetically programmed to mature at rather small sizes.

Onion sets are best used to produce green onions, also called scallions, which can be planted quite early.

Before you plant, know that different varieties of hybrid onions form large bulbs at different maturity dates. They are sold as "short-day," "long-day," and "intermediate-day" varieties, respectively. To grow them, you must start from well-grown seedlings. You can order onion seedlings from specialty growers at 60 to 100 seedlings per bunch.

This compact variety of cucumber is suitable for growing in a smaller garden (top). Big sweet slicing onions are grown from seedlings, not sets (bottom).

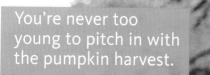
You're never too young to pitch in with the pumpkin harvest.

 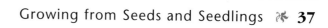

Understanding Your Soil

Eons ago, wildly varying weather, tectonic drift, erosion, wind, glaciers, and volcanic activity helped create the amazing diversity of soil found throughout North America. So diverse, in fact, that a soil map for your state would probably resemble an abstract painting full of splashes and smears of different colors, each representing the arrangement of topsoil, subsoil, and base rock that Mother Nature bestowed on your area.

It's very likely, however, that the builder of your house rearranged these naturally occurring layers by bulldozing trees and hills and spreading the subsoil over the topsoil.

This construction-altered soil is fine for growing trees and shrubs. But food gardens place extreme demands on soil, requiring that you add organic amendments and plant nutrients if you want your garden to be the most productive.

Many beginning gardeners simply dig up their soil, add fertilizers, and plant seeds, only to experience disappointment.

Others mistakenly conclude that their soil is hopeless and purchase topsoil, which can require just as much work and may be infested with weed and grass seeds. (See Chapter 2, page 30 for a step-by-step guide to preparing your garden plot for the very first time.)

In this chapter, we will discuss what soil is, the basic soil types and how to recognize them, how organisms in the soil work to aid plant growth, the different types of soil amendments, and what you can do to get your particular type of soil to function at peak productivity.

Soil Structure and Texture

Soil is composed of two types of particles: mineral and organic. Forget about the rocks; you're going to rake them out.

Mineral particles range from the smallest (clay), to the largest (sand). In between clay and sand are very fine, gritty particles called silt. The term *texture* describes the feel of soil particles when you rub them between your thumb and fingers. (See below.)

Organic particles come in several sizes and various stages of decomposition. In a healthy soil, microorganisms help to glue together (the technical term is *flocculate*) mineral and organic particles into clusters that are separated by air spaces. This arrangement allows good internal drainage and permits air to penetrate into the root zone. The combination of mineral and organic particles, along with the degree of clustering, determine the "structure" of the soil.

Rows of cabbages and shallots grow beautifully in garden soil made rich with plant nutrients and organic amendments.

Silty Soils

Detecting a silty soil is more difficult because you have to gauge by feel the relative size of gritty particles. If they're small, around the same size, and gritty, yet don't have the sharp-edged feel of play sand, you may have silt. Because silts are usually deposited by floodwaters or by the drying up of ancient lakes, they're usually found in isolated areas and are often mixed with clay or sand. Silt tends to fill up the air spaces in soil and make it slow to absorb water and to drain. Silty soils tend to dry hard and resist water penetration. They need to be amended with organic matter in order to be productive.

Sandy Soils

Sandy soils are easy to work and might seem to be ideal for growing vegetables and small fruit. However, they dry out rapidly and can't hold many nutrients or much moisture in reserve. When soil nutrients are added, they tend to drain down through sandy soils to lower layers. Also, organic amendments can decay more rapidly during the summer when the sun heats up the soil. Consequently, organic amendments need to be added to sandy soils more frequently, about every year or two. By the way, a silt loam soil that includes fractional amounts of clay and sand is the first choice of most commercial vegetable growers; only highly organic "muck" soils are more valued by gardeners who sell their produce.

CLAY *and Clay Loam Soils*

SOIL TEXTURE IS BEST DETERMINED by rubbing a bit of moist soil, neither wet or bone dry, between your thumb and forefinger. A clay soil will feel "greasy" when moist

| Sand | Loam | Clay |

Sand (left) is composed of large particles. Clay (right) is made of smaller particles. Loam (center) contains sand and clay and is ideal.

and "cloddy" when dry. You may not find many sand or silt particles in it. However, **when a clay soil contains a significant percentage of sand or silt, it is called a clay loam,** and can be a desirable soil type. Very "heavy" soils have a high percentage of clay particles, drain slowly, and tend to be difficult to work.

But just because it isn't easy to manage doesn't mean you should haul off clay loam soil if that's what you've got on your property. **Replacement soil may require as much labor and expense to make it workable,** and it could be infested with troublesome weed and grass seeds and fleshy, persistent, perennial roots. I would, however, dig out and haul off plastic yellow, gray-blue, or white clay soil. Just imagine trying to garden in Silly Putty and you will understand why. On page 60, I will tell you how to make heavy clay loam soil workable.

Special Western Soils

Arid climates can produce some difficult soils. Chalky, "caliche" soils are common in the Southwest, as are dense, "desert floor" soils. Gardening on caliche soils is complicated by the fact that water rising through the soil by capillary action can become saturated with calcium, magnesium, or other minerals that are deposited in the root zone. Desert floor soils are so dense that heavy iron rods shaped like javelins have to be driven into the soil to break it up enough for a tiller to finish the job. Local garden centers and Master Gardening hotlines can tell you how to prepare and manage these difficult soils.

Even a challenging soil can produce a bountiful harvest.

Life Beneath Your Feet: Microbiota & Macrobiota

The recently coined term, *microbiota* is an all-inclusive name for the microscopic critters in your soil. It includes a great variety of soil organisms: bacterial, fungal, and others with names you may have never heard before. We now know that establishing and maintaining a healthy balance between the many species that make up microbiota, more than fertilizing or watering, is the single most important factor in gardening.

Bacteria, fungi, and nematodes are only a few of the great variety of species at work in the top 8 inches of your soil. Some species live in colonies and work together in what scientists call "symbiotic activity" to nourish plants. These microorganisms are commonly called *mycorrhiza*, and vary according to the genus of

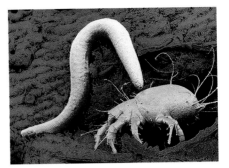

In this microscopic image, a beneficial nematode is investigating a mite to determine if it is good enough to devour.

the plant. Not all plant species require specific mycorrhiza for optimum growth.

Some species of microbiota could be called "grazers." They extract the energy they need to live and reproduce by snacking on dead organic matter in the soil, including the carcasses of microorganisms. Predatory species, on the other hand, get their energy by consuming living organisms. Working together, grazers and predators

TESTING FOR SOIL TYPES: *Texture and Structure*

A FEW SIMPLE TESTS can tell you a great deal about the texture of your soil. Do these tests when the soil is damp, not wet. Dry soil will fall apart, and soggy soil may not crumble.

1 Make a ball of soil, but press only hard enough to make it stick together.

2 Gently bounce the ball up and down in your hands with a rocking motion.

3 Loamy soils crumble partially, sandy soils fall apart, and clay soils stick together.

4 Feel the texture. Sand is gritty, silt feels silky, and clay is slippery.

release essential minerals in the soil or in fertilizer. Some of these organisms surround rootlets the way gloves surround fingers. They absorb plant nutrients and pass them on to rootlets for passage into the vascular (circulatory) system of the plant.

Earthworms and Other Organisms

Without a microscope, you can't see the teeming mass of microscopic animal and vegetable organisms that keep your soil "alive." However, you can see the mass of larger organisms that are called *macrobiota*. Included are the many wriggling or crawling species that live in the soil, and some that spend part of their life cycle as flying insects. Earthworms, beetles, bugs (there is a difference), millipedes, pill bugs, springtails, and spiders are only a few of the species included in macrobiota. Most of these species are predatory, but some graze on succulent fungi and decaying organic matter. In turn, species of microbiota graze on the leftovers. (It's a jungle down there!)

Well-Aerated, Well-Drained Soil

Beneficial bacteria and several other microorganisms require good levels of oxygen in the soil and are described as *aerobic*. To keep them healthy, garden soil needs to be well aerated and porous enough to allow moderately fast drainage. When soil remains soggy for extended periods, anaerobic fungi—which function best when oxygen levels are low—take over, and garden

The channels that earthworms create remain in place after the earthworms have moved on. These channels provide an easy path for both air and water.

plants can suffer and die. Soil turns sour, and you can actually smell the fermentation that is taking place.

It is indeed possible to modify your soil so that it drains well and supplies good levels of oxygen, yet retains sufficient water to sustain plants for several days. In this chapter I will tell you what you need to add to the soil to reach this near-optimum level of drainage and aeration. Do not expect to achieve this magic balance in garden soil right away. Your particular soil may need at least two or three years to rebuild itself, once you have completed the initial tilling or spading that is necessary to begin its conversion from plain old dirt to productive, healthy, and balanced garden soil.

Asparagus thrive in sandy soil.

Marigolds planted alongside asparagus and other crops help control nematodes (above).

Soil Conditioners

Soil conditioners, or *amendments*, are either organic or mineral and are worked into soil to open up its structure to improve drainage and aeration. Organic conditioners improve soil structure by increasing the activity of microorganisms that glue together small particles into clusters. Technical terms for this process are *aggregation* and *flocculation*. The "gluing" promotes aeration and the movement of water both in and out of the soil. Organic conditioners also provide food for microorganisms that thrive on the energy produced as they break it down.

Conditioners vs. fertilizers. Soil conditioners, unlike fertilizers, are not a primary source of concentrated plant nutrients. All organic conditioners do contribute a significant amount of nitrogen (if slowly) and minor amounts of phosphate, potash, and micronutrients. Conditioners do not require an analysis of nutrients or a "derived from" statement on labels.

Particles of organic amendments should range from thumbnail-sized down to the consistency of coffee grounds. Particles that are too fine, such as dust, tend to filter down through soil and collect in layers that impede drainage. Particles that are too large, such as wood chips, can open up the soil too much, causing it to dry out. They can also create "nitrogen drawdown," in which microorganisms draw on nitrogen in the soil for nourishment while they are breaking down the chips. Plants growing on such soils can suffer obvious yellowing, a sign of nitrogen deficiency. Yellowing can be alleviated with nitrogen fertilizer but can recur until the large particles are decomposed.

Counting our several flowerbeds as well as my food garden, my partner and I use about 6 cubic yards of soil conditioner per year. We are fortunate to have access to stable litter from a nearby horse barn and a landscaper who will deliver it in a dump truck. We order two years' worth at a time to reduce hauling costs. One kind of litter is composed of horse manure mixed with sawdust and alfalfa hay; the other is manure mixed with straw. The latter requires composting for a year or two before use. Composting sprouts most of the weed seeds present in horse manure while the seeds are in the pile. Of the two composts, I prefer the manure-sawdust litter because of its finer texture.

Composting can get complicated. Ideally, I should be using more homemade compost, but my pile takes two or three years to break down to usable material. I know that more green matter would speed the process, but I don't collect lawn clippings. Rather, I use a mulching mower and leave the clippings in place. I don't fertilize my lawn because we have a pond downslope and I don't want to pollute it with fertilizer runoff. I don't turn my compost either: that sort of labor is for younger folk. Instead, I let nature take its course and wait until the pile has settled and lost volume from passive composting; then I spread the rough compost as a mulch on aisles in my food garden. This speeds its decomposition. Within a year I can rake it over existing beds to make room in the aisles for more rough compost.

I am ambivalent about raking leaves and moving them into my compost pile. For the health of the trees, I should be running a mulching mower over the dry leaves and allowing them to compost in place. That is what I do on most of my trees, except for the ones close to the house.

Homemade compost bins made from free wood pallets.

SMART *Gardener*

Back when wood was treated with chromated copper arsenate, I advised gardeners to shroud it using plastic sheeting when growing food crops. Now that the chemical used in treating wood no longer contains chromium or arsenic, I'm less worried about the metals being absorbed by food crops. You can still shroud timbers if you'd prefer that your food crops not be exposed to copper.

Piles of yard waste obtained at the municipal dump make good, inexpensive mulch for your garden.

Types of Soil Conditioners

Soil conditioners are available at garden centers in plastic bags and bales and can also be purchased at municipal composting centers. If you are purchasing large quantities, it makes sense to use a local source, because long-distance shipping can be expensive. This is one reason why peat moss is frequently used in Northeast gardens. (Major peat bogs are nearby, in Canada's maritime provinces.) Peat moss is also shipped to west coast and northern Great Plains states from bogs in the central Canadian provinces.

Double-ground pine bark, produced from southern yellow pine, and ground and composted cotton bolls are popular soil conditioners in the South. Pulverized pine and fir bark, produced from western tree species, are often used as conditioners in West Coast and Intermountain states. Rice hulls composted with chicken manure are available in the South and West. Bagged cattle manure—dry, virtually odorless, and nearly weed-free—is widely available. Remember, cattle manure is not a fertilizer; it is a soil conditioner.

Shredded municipal yard waste, while inexpensive, is usually too coarse for use as a soil conditioner. Consider it for mulching instead. Occasionally, double-ground yard waste—passed twice through a grinder—is available. It makes an excellent soil conditioner, especially after a few months of composting.

SOIL *Solutions*

THERE ARE A VARIETY OF WAYS to fix problem soil. Some methods improve the structure of the soil; others feed the plants directly by providing nutrients. Here are the most common.

1. Soil conditioners and amendments. Usually organic materials, such as compost, that improve soil texture by aerating the soil and feeding microorganisms. See opposite.

2. Mulches. Spread on the surface, mulches suppress weeds and limit evaporation of moisture from the soil. When they decompose, they feed microorganisms. Common mulches include wood chips and compost. See page 48.

3. Fertilizers. A variety of organic or inorganic materials deliver nutrients to plant roots. Byproducts of fish processing and bottled liquid concentrates are common types. See page 52.

4. Green manures. These plants are grown and then turned under to supply nutrients to the soil. They include alfalfa and common grasses. See page 58.

Mineral Soil Conditioners and Mulches

Technically speaking, minerals such as limestone, sulfur, and aluminum sulfate are also soil conditioners. Primarily, they are worked into the soil to raise or lower soil pH. Gypsum (calcium sulfate) is occasionally touted as a soil conditioner for breaking up clay. It works on some types of clay but not on others. Overall, organic matter makes a more dependable soil conditioner.

The relative permanence of mineral soil conditioners such as Permatill, which is slate expanded under heat and pressure, make them attractive, but they can be expensive because of shipping costs. Consequently, Permatill is rarely used in food gardens outside of the Southeast where it is mined and processed. A similar material, Haydite, is available in the Midwest.

Why sand is not a good soil conditioner. During my lecturing days, I was often asked about using sand to break up clay. I would then have to explain that while clay soil dries into bricks, sandy clay dries into sandy bricks. Clay is composed of so many fine particles that it tends to overpower any mineral additive. Its effect is so dominant that even if clay amended with sand contains only 25 percent clay; it will act much like pure clay. This is why organic soil conditioners, rather than sand, are preferred for modifying clay. The action of soil organisms opens up clay by "gluing" particles together into clusters rather than by mechanical means. As the clusters form, they leave open spaces throughout the soil for the passage of air and moisture.

You can mulch aisles using gravel or crushed rock, providing you grade your garden site so that excess rainfall can drain away rather than collect beneath the mulch. You will also want to box in your planting beds using treated wood timbers or concrete blocks 6 to 8 inches in height. The boxing will keep gravel out of your planting beds and soil out of the graveled pathways. One of the continuing problems with gravel mulches is the unavoidable spillage of soil onto the gravel walks, where it tends to provide a seedbed for weeds.

Economic, Cosmetic, and Olfactory Considerations

When you calculate the cost of adding a significant amount of soil conditioner to your soil, you may suffer from sticker shock. For example, if you wish to improve the soil in a 500 square foot garden by mixing in 3 inches of soil conditioner, a simple way to figure it would be to calculate 500 x .25 = 125 cubic feet, or a little more than four cubic yards. One cubic yard equals 27 cubic feet. Most bags contain 3 cubic feet of conditioner, so you would need about 42 bags to cover the soil 3 inches deep. Three cubic yards of conditioner would fit into a long-bed pickup truck. Most garden centers offer delivery service on bulk amounts. Be aware that they may require a minimum order larger than your immediate needs, so you might wish to over-order and stockpile the surplus for improving the soil in ornamental borders or lawns. Whoever does the transport should plan on lashing a tarp tightly over the load, or wind could suck much of the conditioner out during the delivery run.

Peat moss is so dry when bagged or baled that it should be moistened while it is still in the plastic packaging. If you try to work dry peat moss into the soil, you may create pockets of bone-dry matter that will persist throughout the growing season and beyond. Small bales of compressed peat moss contain about 3.8 cubic feet. When fluffed, they expand to about twice that volume.

Finding a place to dump a load of soil conditioner can be a problem in developed properties. Fences, hedges, and mushy lawns may prevent dumping the load where it's needed. Be prepared to wheelbarrow it to your food garden site before it blows around or starts getting tracked into the house.

Compost and sand are used for modifying soil.

Moisten peat moss while it is still in the package to avoid dry pockets in your garden.

Mulches

Mulches suppress weeds, decrease evaporation, and nourish soil organisms as they decompose. The type of mulch you choose depends on where you plan to use it. In a fruit orchard, for example, organic mulches can vary from chipped or shredded hardwood, to pine bark, straw, and hay. In food gardens, mulches are used primarily in aisles, where they keep weeds at bay and make pathways walkable after a rain.

Mulches in the food garden. Some gardeners like to reverse their aisles and planting beds when the aisle mulch has decomposed sufficiently to be mixed with the soil as an amendment. This is why hardwood bark, cotton-boll compost, and other mulches that break down rapidly are best in food gardens. Hay is not a suitable food-garden mulch because it is often infested with grass and weed seeds. Straw can be used occasionally, such as for tucking under sweet potato runners and the running vines of squash. Chipped wood breaks down too slowly, and can spoil the fine-textured soils in planting beds if mixed with them.

Finally, after you have some experience with carrots, parsley, and onions, which are slow to sprout and grow, you will see that fine-textured seedbeds of well-conditioned garden soil will produce optimum germination and growth when you cover seeds using a thin layer of coarse sand to prevent crusting of the soil.

A CHICKEN LITTER *Tale*

FEW SOIL CONDITIONERS CREATE A BAD SMELL, even when wet. However, animal manures, or products composted with animal manures, can develop a temporary barnyard smell after a rain. Many years ago, when I was gardening in west Tennessee, I had a load of chicken litter (wood shavings mixed with chicken manure) dumped on a corner of my front lawn. I planned to wheelbarrow it to a food garden site several yards away. Before I could spread it, I was called away on a business trip, and a heavy rain soaked the pile, causing it to form a crust. When I returned, I dug through the crust to get at the dry interior, and was overwhelmed by the stench. I came into the house muttering about "gagging a maggot," stripped off my reeking clothes, showered, and arranged for a strong teenage boy to do the dirty work. He bravely moved one wheelbarrow load and was overcome with retching. I paid him double for his time and attacked the job myself. Even for someone raised on a farm and accustomed to shoveling out chicken houses, that job was an ordeal. Thankfully, my home was the first built in the development, and the odor from the spread litter dissipated before it created a panic in other neighborhoods. By the way, the garden produced prodigiously, thanks to the chicken litter.

In the two food gardens shown here, finely-ground wood chips are used to suppress weeds around plants (above, left) and to create a curved garden walkway (above, right). Mulch that is filled with large chunks or sticks is not suitable for a food garden.

A GREAT VARIETY OF MATERIALS can be used for mulches in the aisles of food gardens. My favorite is ground hardwood bark. I buy a dump-truck load at a time. It is attractive, doesn't blow or wash away, and gives me all-weather, mud-free access to the garden. In the Midwest, hardwood bark mulch is more plentiful than pine bark mulch, and usually less expensive. In the South, ground cotton bolls make good mulch.

Cedar, cypress, and eucalyptus mulches are available in a few places. Cedar and cypress decompose a bit slower than hardwood bark and cost more. Ecologically speaking, the cutting of young, native bald cypress trees for grinding into mulches should be forbidden, but isn't. Almost all mature cypress trees have long since been harvested for timber, and replacement trees should be protected for future timber production, not cut for grinding. However, we should cheer the cutting and grinding of invasive eucalyptus trees to make way for native tree species.

From an ecological standpoint, **shredded and roughly composted yard waste** is one of the best mulches, even though it might contain occasional pieces of plastic or metal. A few cities compost yard waste with sewage sludge, speeding the process using heated aeration. The hot composting makes the finished material safe to use. When put through a shredder twice after composting, yard waste is fine-textured enough for use as food garden or landscape bed soil conditioner. Common, single-shredded, composted yard waste tends to contain many chunks of wood. You may wish to pile such mulch for a year or two to break down these large pieces.

Straw mulch should be used within an enclosure. For several days after application, before rain or irrigation settles it in place, strong winds can pick up straw and blow it all over the landscape. You can stop the straw from spreading by laying newspapers over the entire food garden. **Don't substitute hay for straw.** While straw is comparatively weed-free, hay is loaded with seeds of grass and broad-leaved weeds. Straw mulch is good for spreading around plants such as strawberries and squash, as it reduces the rotting of fruit by contact with soil.

Pinestraw (pine needles) is available in the South and to a limited extent in the West. It makes an attractive mulch but is expensive for use on a food garden. **Peat moss does not make good mulch,** despite being an excellent soil conditioner. When spread atop the soil, it tends to form a crust that repels rain and sprinkler irrigation. This applies to peat humus as well. Peat humus is harvested from older deposits that lie beneath sphagnum peat moss in bogs and is usually darker in color.

Black plastic mulches can reduce evaporation and suppress weeds. They work best in hardiness Zone 3, where they can be used in combination with clear plastic tunnel houses stretched over hoops. The retained heat and frost protection make it possible for far-northern and northwestern coastal growers to produce eggplants, peppers, and slicing tomatoes. In warmer climates, black plastic mulches tend to trap so much heat and soil moisture that root zone pathogens can multiply rapidly and kill plants. Ecologically, it is difficult to justify the use of black plastic mulches, especially when it is time to dispose of them.

Spoiled hay mulch

Chopped leaf mulch

Dried grass clippings mulch

Wheat straw mulch

Southern pine needle mulch

Black plastic mulch

Long-Term Considerations

Expect organic soil conditioners and mulches to decompose completely after three or four years, faster in warm, humid climates. If you look at mulch as an investment in soil improvement, you can rationalize the cost and effort of replacement. As mulch decomposes, earthworms take it down into the root zone of plants where it contributes to soil fertility. You might also consider "no-till gardening." Rather than digging up the soil each fall or spring, you spread fine-textured soil conditioner over the bed at the onset of winter. For a more detailed explanation of no-till gardening, see Chapter 9, page 164.

This home gardener is spreading wood fireplace ash, a fine-particled source of plant nutrients and minerals, onto a bed of shallots.

The GOOD, the BAD, and the UGLY

BACK WHEN I WAS A PRESENTER on the original PBS series, *Victory Garden*, our TV crew visited a large food garden in Aurora, Colorado. The owner had **laid down strips of used carpeting as a mulch between rows of vegetables.** Because of the dry climate, the carpet helped to reduce evaporation without interfering with sprinkler irrigation. I have also seen **dried lawn clippings spread over two or three layers of newspaper,** and have personally tried mulches of straw with considerable success. So much depends on the visibility of your food garden from the street or from neighbors' yards. You don't want to create unsightly, smelly, or toxic mulch. **Grass clippings should always be dried before spreading,** and not used at all for mulching if the grass has been sprayed using a selective weed killer. Drying lawn clippings before adding them to compost reduces the chance of them settling into a slippery, smelly mess.

Make certain that leaves and grass clippings are thoroughly dry before using them as mulch in your food garden.

SOIL AMENDMENTS AND FERTILIZERS derived from natural sources often contain much more than simply mineral nutrients. The table below lists some of their other benefits, as well as giving application rates.

MATERIAL	Primary Benefits	Analysis (N-P-K, plus minor & trace nutrients)	Average Application Rate per 1,000 sq. ft. when Soils Test:			Notes
			Low	Moderate	Adequate	
Alfalfa meal	Organic matter, nitrogen	5-1-2	50 lbs.	35 lbs.	25 lbs.	Contains a natural growth stimulant plus trace elements
Aragonite	Calcium	96% calcium carbonate	100 lbs.	50 lbs.	25 lbs.	Can replace limestone
Calcitic lime		65-80% calcium carbonate 3-15% magnesium carbonate	Use soil test; quantity depends on soil type as well as pH			Use in soils with adequate magnesium and low calcium
Colloidal phosphate	Phosphate	0-2-2	60 lbs.	25 lbs.	10 lbs.	Adds to soil reserves as well as available quantity
Compost	Organic matter, soil life	0.5-0.5-0.5 to 3-3-3	200 lbs.	100 lbs.	50 lbs.	Adds balanced nutrients & the microbiota to make them available
Dolomitic lime	Calcium, magnesium	51% calcium carbonate 40% magnesium carbonate	Use soil test; quantity depends on soil type as well as pH			Use in soils with low magnesium and low calcium
Epsom salts	Magnesium, sulfur	10% magnesium, 13% sulfur	5 lbs.	3 lbs.	1 lb.	Use when magnesium is so low that other sources won't work
Fish emulsion	Nitrogen	4-1-1; 5% sulfur	2 oz.	1 oz.	1 oz.	Can be used as a foliar feed too, mix 50/50 with liquid seaweed, and dilute to half the recommended strength
Granite meal	Potash, trace elements	4% total potash; 67% silicas, 19 trace elements	100 lbs.	50 lbs.	25 lbs.	Rock powders add to long-term soil fertility and health
Greensand	Potash, trace elements	7% potash, 32 trace minerals	100 lbs.	50 lbs.	25 lbs.	Excellent potash source
Kelp meal	Potash, trace elements	1.5-0.5-2.5	20 lbs.	10 lbs.	5 lbs.	Best for spot applications where extra potash is needed
Rock phosphate	Phosphate	0-3-3; 32% calcium, 11 trace elements	60 lbs.	25 lbs.	10 lbs.	Apply when you start the garden and every four years once soil phosphate levels are adequate
Soybean meal	Nitrogen	7-0.5-2.3	50 lbs.	25 lbs.	10 lbs.	Excellent soil amendment during the second half of the season
Sul-Po-Mag	Sulfur, potash, magnesium	0-0-22; 11% magnesium, 22% sulfur	10 lbs.	7 lbs.	5 lbs.	Use only if magnesium levels are low & never with dolomitic lime
Worm castings	Organic matter	0.5-0.5-0.3	n/a	n/a	n/a	Use in potting soils and for spot fertilizing

Fertilizers and Plant Nutrients

As we've seen, a number of products and processes must work together to create a successful first garden and to build productivity over the years. Understanding the various factors involved is a continuing challenge for gardeners. Here's how fertilizers and plant nutrients fit into the big picture.

Fertilizers and plant nutrients are not the same.

Think of fertilizers as the vehicles for delivering nutrients to the soil. The soil then delivers these nutrients to plants in forms that can be absorbed by their roots. Plant nutrients are either *major* (essential) or *micro* (trace elements). The three major plant nutrients are *nitrogen, phosphate,* and *potash*. These are listed by percentage and weight on all fertilizer packaging. Micronutrients are usually added to fertilizer sold in liquid forms. Laws do not require their percentages to be listed on fertilizer analyses, but they are usually mentioned as a sales advantage.

Yellow squash fresh-picked from the garden makes a delicious and healthful addition to the family dinner table.

Plant a garden of mixed salad greens.

SHOPPING FOR
Food Garden Fertilizers

VISIT ANY MAJOR GARDEN CENTER, and you will find a bewildering array of brands and formulations of fertilizers. Here's how you can winnow through them to find what you need.

1. **Avoid lawn fertilizers;** they are too high in nitrogen for tomatoes and peppers.

2. Consider the granular inorganic fertilizers such as 10-10-10 or 13-13-13, often called **"corn fertilizers,"** but only for the first time you prepare the soil. Thereafter, switch to granular organic fertilizers for maintaining soil fertility. They are easier on soil organisms than the harsh chemical compounds in processed fertilizers.

3. You won't find many brands of **granular organic fertilizers** and they will be considerably more expensive than granular processed or inorganic fertilizers. When you compare, you will be paying even more per pound

of actual nutrients than you would with inorganic fertilizers. But don't despair: processed chicken manures are coming on the market; they combine relatively high analysis with more attractive price levels.

4. **If your plants are yellowing and you want them to green up, consider a water-soluble liquid fertilizer.** Buy the crystals and dilute them as per the directions. Avoid the pre-diluted brands: the water in them is as expensive as the bottled water in an airport.

5. Don't rely on liquid fertilizers for your basic nutrient supply; they are like a shot in the arm, and their effect lasts only a few days. Some of the liquid fertilizers are labeled "organic" but may be spiked with chemicals to raise the content of nitrogen and phosphate. I have found that when I use granular organic fertilizers with the "no-till" garden method (see Chapter 9, page 164), I rarely have to resort to liquid plant foods.

A steaming pile of compost for making raised beds.

Organic Fertilizers

Organic fertilizers fulfill the age-old wisdom to "feed the soil rather than the plants." Although this advice came long before scientists understood why it is sound practice to do so, many now agree that feeding the soil is valid. If you keep soil healthy by "feeding" it organic soil conditioners and organic fertilizers, it will in turn feed your plants. However, some technicians, and many home gardeners, still prefer to apply processed fertilizers because of their predictability and efficiency. Further along in this book, you may find me referring to feeding plants. Old habits die hard.

Organic fertilizers are usually derived from the waste stream produced by food production facilities, animal feedlots, and stables. But supplies of the raw materials that are available to fertilizer manufacturers are drying up. Canning and freezing facilities for fish, shellfish, and mollusks are converting more of their waste into food for the very species they process, and more byproducts, such as beef, pork, and chicken trimmings, are going into pet foods. Asian countries are purchasing some of the meats that are not marketed here. Cottonseed and soybean meals, both excellent fertilizers, are becoming prohibitively expensive.

Organic fertilizers come in three basic forms: dry granular, liquid concentrate, and ready-to-use liquid nutrient sources. The ready-to-use sources are the most expensive by far. Why pay for shipping water from a manufacturing plant to your garden when you can dissolve concentrated sources using tap water?

Many brands of concentrated liquid organic fertiliz-

PRAISE the Cricket

BRICKO FARMS in Augusta, Georgia, distributes a fertilizer that I have used with success for many years. It is sold as Kricket Krap and, all kidding aside, it is pure cricket manure. The crickets are fed several kinds of organic byproducts. The end result contains 25 percent protein. Being so powerful, it must be used as directed. If you are curious about how and where one would get cricket manure, crickets are grown by the millions on specialized farms around Augusta for fish bait and pet food. The crickets are grown in cages with catch-trays. The manure is dry and meal-like in texture. It makes manure tea that can make your plants sit up and whistle Dixie.

SMART Gardener

You may wonder why the terms "phosphate" and "potash" are used on fertilizer packaging rather than the standard names for these chemical elements, phosphorus and potassium. The answer is that those stand-alone elements must be bonded with other base substances to make them stable enough to handle safely.

ers are byproducts of fish processing. They offer the benefit of complex organic compounds as well as moderate, but adequate, levels of nitrogen, phosphate, potash, and micronutrients. A processor of farm-raised catfish in Mississippi *hydrolyzes* fish scraps to produce a product that's effective, yet virtually free of the fishy odor that so often follows the application of many of the better-known fish fertilizers.

Read the label. It is worth repeating that the analysis of granular organic fertilizers on labels is misleading, and not by intent. Organic fertilizers require the action of soil microorganisms for the breakdown and release of nitrogen, phosphate, and potash, along with beneficial, complex organic compounds. Most organic fertilizers are rather slow and gentle in reaction, but chicken and sheep manure are exceptions. Unless mixed with an organic carrier, chicken or sheep manure can be so "hot" that it can burn plant roots. The term "hot" refers to the quick release of ammonia and salts during breakdown.

On the plus side, methods are being refined to process poultry manure into safe-to-use, nonodoriferous fertilizer. Sheep manure has long been used as a mild fertilizer despite its lingering odor. Dried cattle manure, while too weak to be considered a fertilizer, does work well when used as a soil conditioner.

If you are determined to use strictly organic fertilizers, you should read the "derived from" information on labels. Some formulations are "juiced up" using di-ammonium phosphate to boost the nitrogen and phosphate numbers on the analysis. Three of the best-known sources of brand-name organic fertilizers are Bradfield Organics, Espoma, and Milorganite.

Certain mail-order catalogs and independent garden centers in large cities specialize in organic fertilizers and pest controls. Large, independent garden centers often have organic fertilizers packaged for their customers under a private label. Personally, I prefer to use organic fertilizers instead of mineral, but only in developed countries do gardeners have that choice.

Mineral Fertilizers

Mineral fertilizers are usually processed to boost their percentage of major nutrient elements. This processing consumes much more energy, as does the grinding and pelletizing of raw or processed materials to simplify mixing or handling. Such fertilizers are maligned by some organic gardeners and are blamed for poisoning soil. That situation exists in only a miniscule number of fields owned by commercial growers, and in most cases can be rectified by flooding the field to leach away accumulated salts. A more serious problem with processed fertilizers, especially those applied to lawns, commercial turf, and row-crop farmland is their tendency to wash into ponds and waterways along with valuable topsoil.

As I mentioned, organic fertilizers are my first choice in the food garden, and I am glad that I am afforded the luxury of choosing to use them instead of mineral fertilizers. To me, it seems counterproductive to criticize mineral fertilizers when they are vital to feeding people and animals worldwide. Many societies have to burn most of the available organic matter to cook meals and heat homes. Growing and turning under green manure crops is out of the question; they need to grow food crops on every square inch of arable land to produce enough to stay alive. They require mineral fertilizer to maintain productivity in their soil, even when it has to be shipped in.

Granular, Processed Fertilizers

More packaged fertilizers than any other are the granular, processed type, and lawn fertilizers dominate. Most of these fertilizers are too high in nitrogen content for

Acorn squash thrives in a rich, well-drained soil.

CHEMICAL *vs* ORGANIC

I MAINTAIN THAT THE DISPUTE between advocates of chemical and organic fertilizers is unnecessary. Both chemical and organic fertilizers are needed, and home gardeners should be encouraged to use in moderation whichever works best for them without being subjected to criticism. Further, the manufacturers of chemical fertilizers should not have to face roadblocks thrown up by overzealous organic gardeners. **Laws are in place to limit the environmental impact of fertilizer manufacturing processes.** Their industry is one of the most heavily regulated and monitored in the USA. We need to think globally to reduce the number of people suffering from malnutrition. As for the energy used in producing mineral fertilizers, bear in mind that much energy is also used in grinding and hauling organic soil conditioners and mulches. It is extremely difficult to raise or maintain levels of organic matter in the soil using just the output of a home compost heap fed with trimmings, clippings, and leaves. Supplementary sources of organic matter are needed.

feeding vegetables. Unless they are *side-dressed* into the soil, meaning trickled into furrows alongside rows of plants and covered over with soil, the release of ammonia and salts can burn roots.

Some include herbicides in their formulation and should not be used on food crops or ornamentals. Other fertilizers mention "acid forming" in their promotional copy. These are suitable for blueberries, currants, and gooseberries, but not for general use on food crops.

Magnesium sulfate, sold as Epsom salts, is often used but seldom recommended as a booster for tomatoes, peppers, eggplant, and roses. Epsom salts works on some soils but not on others. This may explain why Epsom salts are rarely recommended in state extension service bulletins on growing vegetables. Magnesium is a secondary nutrient and is not usually deficient in soils, unless they are acid in pH. Epsom salts are usually used at a concentration of one-half cup dissolved in 8 quarts of warm water.

Crystalline and Liquid Concentrates of Processed Fertilizers

Some of the most familiar brands of fertilizers are crystalline or liquid. Scott's Miracle-Gro 15-30-15 is probably the best-known water-soluble, crystalline fertilizer formulation. Schultz and Peters make different liquid or crystalline formulations for various specialty plants, including vegetables. Numerous regional processors package proprietary, liquid-feeding products. All produce a shot-in-the-arm response—quick but short-lived. You could liquid-feed vegetables twice weekly, using recommended concentrations, and not over-stimulate plants, but much of the nutrient value would be wasted.

Plastic-Coated, Controlled-Release Fertilizers (CRF)

Used for many years by commercial growers of containerized nursery stock, plastic-coated, controlled-release fertilizers (CRF) subsequently became widely available to home gardeners. When mixed with potting soils, they can feed for three to nine months, depending on the thickness of the plastic coating and the prevailing soil temperature. Given normal watering frequency, plants in containers will be fed at a rate consistent with their seasonal needs, meaning, at a low rate during cool months, and a higher rate during warm months.

Another benefit of CRFs is their efficiency—relatively little of their nutrient content is lost in drainage water as *leachate*. However, CRFs are simply too expensive to use on most food crops growing in the ground. The one exception is with sandy soil, where granular or water-soluble fertilizers leach away quickly. High-value food crops such as strawberries and blueberries can also justify their use.

Osmocote was the first CRF to be introduced. I was involved in its introduction more than 30 years ago. Since that time, several competitive coated fertilizers have been put on the market. All of them work well for feeding plants in containers.

DO *the Math*

SOIL TESTS RESULTS are often stated in terms developed for farmers, not for home gardeners. For example, the amounts of nitrogen, phosphate, and potash needed to reach optimum productivity may be listed at "pounds per 1,000 square feet." The easy way to convert these figures for your home garden is to divide the pounds by 10, which will give you the amount per 100 square feet, (10 feet x 10 feet), roughly the size of a small room.

Soils labs will ask you what you will be planting in your soil—for example, a food garden, flowers, or a lawn—then make their fertilizer recommendations accordingly. But you will need to get out your calculator. **After deciding which kind and analysis of fertilizer you want to use, you will need to figure how much to apply in order to meet the amounts suggested by the lab.** For example, the lab may tell you that your proposed food garden will need 10 pounds each of nitrogen, phosphate, and potash, per 1,000 square feet. That converts to 1 pound each of nitrogen, phosphate, and potash per 100 square feet.

Organic fertilizers are typically low in analysis. Let's consider one with an analysis of 2-3-3, for example. How much would you need to apply per 100 square feet to meet the recommendations listed above? The answer isn't precise, because the numbers in the analysis are unequal. You would need to apply approximately one-third pound (let's call it 5 ounces) per 100 square feet. This would be spot-on for

An urban community garden in Spain.

the phosphate and potash. But you have shorted the nitrogen somewhat. You would need to bump up the amount to 8 ounces of organic fertilizer per 100 square feet. You will be adding a bit too much phosphate and potash, but plants have some capacity for luxury consumption beyond their need for healthy growth. Because it is organic, the slight excess won't burn plant roots.

Green Manures

Doubtless you have heard what Bess Truman allegedly said about President Harry: "It took me 30 years to get him to say manure."

Today, the phrase *green manure* rolls off the tongues of many food gardeners. Green manures are special crops grown expressly for chopping and turning under, serving the same purpose as animal manure. They are especially valuable for enhancing the population of ben-eficial organisms, both large and small, and serve primarily as a slow-release source of nitrogen. Unlike animal manures, they are not alkaline in reaction and do not release ammonia. Green manure crops should be annuals. Annuals will not regrow strongly when mowed and turned under. They can be grown on a portion of your food garden that can be spared from production for an entire season; they can be seeded among standing crops in late summer; or they can be planted in strips between food crops in large gardens.

COVER CROPS *and* GREEN MANURES

CROP	Lifecycle	Primary Purpose	Seeding Rate lb./1,000 sq. ft.*	Planting Time	Time to Turn Under	Soil Type
Alfalfa *Medicago sativa*	Perennial	Contributes nitrogen	3	Spring	After 2 years	pH 6.5–7; well-drained
Buckwheat *Fagopyrum esculentum*	Annual	Contributes phosphorus/ smothers weeds	3	Early-mid summer	Late summer-early fall	Widely adaptable
Clover, Dutch white *Trifolium repens*	Perennial	Contributes nitrogen	0.25	Spring-late summer	Fall or following year if at all	pH 6.5–7; well-drained
Clover, Mammoth red *Trifolium pratense*	Biennial	Contributes nitrogen	0.5	Spring-fall	After 1–2 years	Well-drained, tolerates pH of 6.0 if limed at seeding
Clover, Crimson *Trifolium incarnatum*	Annual	Contributes nitrogen	0.5–0.66	Late summer in south/ spring in north	Late spring in South/ midsummer in north	Well-drained, pH 6.5–7
Marigold, 'Sparky' *Tagetes erecta*	Annual	Controls nematodes	2–3 oz.	Mid-late spring	After flowering	Adaptable
Oats *Avena sativa*	Annual	Prevents erosion	3–4	Early spring or fall	At flowering; winter-kills in north	Adaptable
Peas, field, 'Trapper' *Pisum sativum*	Annual	Contributes nitrogen/ smothers weeds	3	Early spring	After pods form	Well-drained
Rapeseed *Brassica napus*	Annual	Alkalizes soil	3 oz.	Mid-spring	After flowering	Adaptable
Ryegrass *Lolium multiflorum*	Annual	Adds organic matter	2	Early spring-late summer	At flowering; winterkills in north	Adaptable
Sweetclover *Melilotus officinalis*	Biennial	Contributes nitrogen; breaks up hardpan	0.5	Mid spring-summer	After flowering or following spring	pH close to 7, well-drained
Vetch, Hairy *Vicia villosa*	Annual	Contributes nitrogen	1–3	Spring-late summer	After flowering or early following spring	Adaptable
Winter Rye *Lolium*	Annual	Adds organic matter; phytotoxic to weeds	4–6	Spring through mid-fall	At flowering or early following spring	Adaptable

*Decrease seeding rate appropriately when using the seed in a mix.

Winter rye is used as a green manure crop.

Fall-seeded green manure crops serve a dual purpose: they decrease wintertime soil erosion and leaching of nutrients, and when chopped and turned under the following spring, they nourish soil organisms. Annual ryegrass is a popular green manure crop and can be sown in the spring or fall. Buckwheat is usually sown in early to midsummer. In the South, annual crimson clover is favored for late summer or fall seeding.

Allow about a month between turning under green manure crops and planting vegetables. This will give the green matter time to be greatly reduced by decomposition.

Tonics

There are numerous elixirs promoted as a means to improve soil health and to increase productivity. These are neither fertilizers nor soil conditioners, and none can cause a major or lasting improvement in soil. Some of them work—some don't. Some were developed before scientists used electron microscopy to study soil microorganisms.

Older tonic formulations include vitamins, enzymes, and seaweed extracts. Vitamins and enzymes are composed of relatively large molecules that are too big to be absorbed intact by plant roots. They have to be broken down by soil organisms before they become "available" to plant rootlets. Can you provide the same effect for less money by maintaining good levels of organic matter in the soil? The same question could be asked when assessing the benefits of worm castings. They can help improve productivity, but could you achieve the same results by modifying your soil to support more earthworms? Who can say whether seaweed or kelp extract is worth the money? It seems to be effective on crops grown on worn-out soils, but what about soils that are healthy and productive? I've never used any of these products, and so I can't verify their value.

THE SOIL-FOOD WEB

A PROMISING "TONIC," and I use this term only because no precise word exists to describe it, may come out of research being conducted at Oregon State University. There, investigations are being conducted on what they call the "Soil-Food Web." **This term describes the way soil microorganisms and macroorganisms work together to decompose organic matter,** which, in turn, nourishes plants. Together, these processes **increase the uptake of plant nutrients and stimulate plants** through the energy created by the activity of microorganisms, principally beneficial bacteria. These processes have always existed, of course. However, it wasn't until soil scientists could actually see what was going on that they could better understand how plants absorb nutrients and how we can assist microbiota in their vitally important service.

The University is researching machines that produce **highly aerated solutions.** The solution, after 24 hours of aerated bubbling, **teems with beneficial microorganisms.** When sprayed on or sprinkled around plants, it appears to accelerate the release and uptake of available nutrients. The jury is still out on the short- and long-term benefits of these modern compost teas.

New research on the relationship between soil organisms could result in better fertilizers for home gardeners.

Common Soil Problems and How to Fix Them

In my decades of lecturing on gardening, I've heard so many times, "My soil is heavy clay; I just can't work with it," or "My soil is so sandy that it won't hold water and needs frequent additions of fertilizers." Neither of these situations is hopeless by any means. In fact, both types of soil can be made into highly productive gardens.

To help you understand what is needed to improve your soil, think of high-quality potting soil and how it works. Producers of potting soils know to mix certain proportions of pine or fir bark with premium-quality sphagnum peat moss and perhaps a bit of perlite, which is silica expanded by heat and pressure. To this they add limestone to balance the natural acidity of the peat moss, water-soluble fertilizer, and perhaps controlled-release fertilizer. Finally, they add a dash of product to help the dry-as-a-bone mix absorb water, and—voila!—

Hot compost zaps weed seeds.

you have a mix that will permit plants to reach their genetic potential.

Potting soil allows plants to grow so well because it drains at a moderately fast rate. This drains off excess moisture and keeps the soil from becoming soggy. As water drains out, air, including vital oxygen, is drawn into the root zone of plants. Yet potting soil retains enough moisture to sustain plants for a day or two, thanks to the content of peat moss. At the same time,

IMPROVING *Clay and Clay-Loam Soils*

1. Wait until your soil is dry enough to crumble, but not dust-dry, before you turn it over using a spade or tiller. **Working clay while it is wet or parched is self-defeating;** you end up with big, hard clods or dust that puddles and runs together when wet.

2. Work up one small area at a time. Budget for adding at least 2 to 3 inches of organic soil amendment before tillage. Soil conditioners can be expensive but are absolutely necessary for good drainage, aeration, and biological activity. Consider buying them in bulk quantities to save money.

3. **Spread fertilizer and lime according to your soil test recommendations before tilling your soil.**

4. Don't create a bathtub without a drain plug! In your initial soil preparation, use soil excavated from aisles to raise the level of beds for planting. Raised beds will give your plants a moist but not soggy root run.

5. **Every year thereafter, add a 2- to 3-inch layer of organic soil conditioner** to beds at the end of the fall or winter gardening season. Cut furrows or planting holes through it for planting seeds or setting out plants, and you won't need to till your soil again.

When improving clay or clay loam soil, work up one small area at a time.

the water-soluble fertilizer gets the plants off to a fast start before their long-term nutrition is handed over to the controlled-release fertilizers. Gradually, a population of beneficial microorganisms will develop within the root zone.

So, how do you create a happy situation like this in your garden soil? If tests reveal that you have clay soil, see "Improving Clay and Clay-Loam Soils," opposite; if tests indicate sandy soil, see "Improving Sandy Soils," below.

Unusual Soil Types

Some unusual soil types include silt loams, loessial hills, organic muck, shallow soil underlain by rock, chalky *caliche* soils of the Southwest, and desert floor soils. Each of these soil types requires different management to achieve maximum production of vegetables and fruit. Rely on your State Extension Service and local independent garden centers for advice on making them workable and responsive.

IMPROVING
Sandy Soils

WITH SANDY AND SANDY-LOAM SOILS, the challenge is to modify them to hold more moisture and to extend the life of fertilizers by slowing down their drainage due to irrigation or rains.

1. **Select a fine-textured organic soil conditioner,** such as sphagnum peat moss, cotton boll compost, double-ground municipal compost, or rice hulls composted with chicken manure. In the East and Southeast, where soils tend to be acid, dried cow manure is effective. However, on alkaline western soils, an acidic soil conditioner such as peat moss is preferred.

2. **Spread a 3-inch layer of soil conditioner, fertilizer, and lime as recommended by soil tests.** In the East and Southeast you may have to lime your soil every second year. These soils also heat up faster and retain more heat than clay or clay loam soils. This depletes their content of organic matter rapidly.

3. **Raised beds are not helpful in sandy or sandy loam soils** unless they are low-lying and there is a high water table.

THE REAL "DIRT"
on Soil

Root vegetables grow best in soil rich in organic matter.

EXPERIENCED GARDENERS try not to refer to soil as "dirt." To them, dirt is what politicians use in attack ads. Most soils, on the other hand, can be used for growing plants. While soils from various locations can be as different as night and day, all are basically colonies of microbiota that live in or on a structure of mineral and organic particles. **Healthy garden soils support relatively large populations of beneficial bacteria and small populations of fungi and other microscopic plant forms.** By comparison, forest soils support relatively large and varied populations of fungi. Both bacteria and fungi are needed in garden soils. Given good aeration and drainage, they will develop a beneficial mix of species. Soil conditioners and mulches help these beneficial soil organisms to thrive and increase.

All the Tools You Need

Whenever I mentor first-time gardeners involved in community gardening, I usually have to show them how to hold and use common garden tools. That leads to teaching them to recognize weeds so they don't get carried away and take out the good guys while wiping out the bad. Having to begin at the beginning with them is no surprise.

What does surprise me are all the experienced gardeners who are unaware of the many specialized hand tools available to make their chores easier. I see myself as a "minimalist gardener," a holdover from the hard times when my family had to make tools serve multiple uses. Consequently, there are few tools today that I consider truly essential. You will undoubtedly have other favorites, based on your reach, strength, and agility. Other than an ancient two-cylinder gasoline engine that powered a big rotary saw for cutting firewood, my family had no power equipment—no tractor, no tiller, no lawn mower. (No lawn, either.) In fact, we

didn't have electric power until I was 11 years old. We used horses and mules to pull or carry equipment and materials, and added their manure to that shoveled out of the cow barn. Later in my gardening life, I owned tillers, large and small, but no more. I still own power lawn mowers and hedge shears, but keep their manual counterparts on hand to do the job while they are out for repairs. Using sturdy, sharp hand tools for my gardening tasks gives me a fundamental satisfaction that is difficult to describe to non-gardeners, but you will easily understand once you've enjoyed the ease and efficiency they add to your gardening routine.

Preparing Your First Garden

Power Tillers

The only time you will need a tiller in your food garden is when you first prepare the soil for planting. (See "Preparing Your First Garden Plot," Chapter 2, page 30.) Small tillers are not up to the job of pulverizing heavy, compacted soil and incorporating large amounts of soil conditioners. Thus, for that first and only time, rent a big tiller of at least 8 horsepower; then return it when the job is done. That way, you won't have to step around a tiller taking up space in your garage or tool shed year after year. In doing so, you will be bucking centuries of the ancient tradition of tilling the soil.

Not everyone—particularly manufacturers of tillers—will agree that yearly preparation of soil by pulverizing it with a tiller is not a sound practice. Tillage destroys the complex, interdependent colonies of soil organisms known as microbiota and macrobiota. In garden soil that hasn't been tilled or deeply spaded, "good" bacteria keeps harmful bacteria and fungi under control. In such healthy soil, the activity of these beneficial bacteria also helps form the soil into loose clusters and drinking straw-like channels. These structures help the passage of oxygen into the soil and waste gasses out of the soil.

You will need a power tiller only once, so rent it instead of buying one.

Hand Tools

Almost all my hand tools for gardening are old. They show the wear and tear of heavy use. When I can find them, I buy landscaper-grade garden tools. They have substantial steel where the metal meets the soil, heavy-duty sockets, and practically unbreakable straight-grain hardwood or steel handles.

Hoes

One good hoe can replace the three or four types you'll see for sale in hardware stores and by mail order. A square-bladed "chopping hoe" can be used for breaking up clods, for shaving off weeds, and for making furrows for direct-seeding of vegetables. I keep a good-sized metal file handy for honing an edge on my chopping hoe. Although I could get by without them, I also have a stirrup hoe for weeding and a hoe with a triangular blade for opening furrows and weeding in tight spots. If I could find a long-handled "Yankee Weeder" I would jump at the

A "hand claw" rake is useful for dislodging weeds.

Accept the fact that garden soil is very much alive, and is far more than a sponge to hold moisture and an anchor for plant roots. Chapter 3, beginning on page 38, is devoted to understanding garden soils and how to manage them for maximum production. Invest in soil amendments to improve drainage, aeration, and microbiological activity. A mellow, easy-to-work soil can be a joy to work, as well as to watch, as plants respond to your efforts.

The rake and the hoe are the most useful tools in your garden.

chance to buy it. This type of weeder is forged from a strap of steel by bending it into an "L" shape and twisting the cutting blade so that it lies flat on the ground. Both leading and trailing edges of the cutting blade should be kept sharp. You can sneak in between good plants to get at the bad guys and shave them off with a minimum of soil disturbance. By the way, many of the rinky-dink hoes for sale at hardware store are too flimsy to hold up to hard use, green paint notwithstanding.

Use a hand-held trowel for digging small holes for transplanting.

The result of neglecting to properly clean, maintain, and store tools looks woeful and performs even worse.

Spading Forks

These usually have four or five flattened tines. The best ones are either forged from fairly flexible steel and painted, or made from stainless steel. They are designed for digging in soil that is too heavy or sticky for a spade or shovel. They are also great for digging potatoes. Almost all come equipped with "D" handles, but long-handled styles can occasionally be found in catalogs. If you're short on capital for buying tools, put off getting a spading fork—you can get by temporarily using a shovel.

Shovels and Spades

There is a difference between the two. Garden shovels are designed primarily for moving soil from one place to another. The blades of shovels are bent at the shank so that when you slide it on the soil surface, the handle slants up to the level of the gardener's hands. It so happens that shovels with rounded points make mighty good spades when you need to dig planting holes. You might guess that I have little use for garden spades. That is true. To me, a spade with a blade that is parallel with the handle is awkward. The ones with short "D" handles and stainless steel blades and shanks make impressive gifts for gardeners, and they look really snazzy hanging on a rack in a garage. That's where mine stays.

In addition to "D" handles, shovels and spades come with long or short straight handles. Now that I have shrunk to about average height, I find that long handles of hardwood give me the reach and leverage I need when chopping small tree roots, prying up rocks, and digging planting holes. I have a couple of sacrificial shovels with handles made of wooden spools wrapped in yellow PVC. If I broke a handle of ash or hickory I would grieve over it, but would shed no tears over a broken handle on a flimsy tool.

I have to ask for my favorite shovel when I need it. My gardening partner has a cool little "ladies shovel" with a hardwood handle of medium length and a sturdy blade only half the size of my big, manly shovels. It is great for digging small holes for transplanting. She graciously loans it to me. Having to ask keeps me humble, as does returning it to its assigned place.

Spading forks are good for double-digging.

Pitchforks and Manure Forks

Pitchforks have four to six rounded tines with moderately sharp points. They are designed for pitching (moving) hay or piles of weeds. Manure forks are sturdier, with nine or ten tines. As for their use, I find my manure fork indispensable for handling coarse compost or shredded hardwood bark. I use my pitchfork for picking up piles of weeds and prunings. Both types have flexible tines that can be bent back into alignment.

A pitchfork is the best tool for moving manure.

Iron Rakes and Leaf Rakes

A good iron rake is hard to find. Iron rakes are used for smoothing the soil in gardens. Inexpensive iron rakes have a short spike welded on the center of the tined bar. The spike is forced into the end of the wooden handle, clamped in place with a cone of sheet metal, and held in place with a screw. After a few months of use the wood will dry and shrink, and the spike will slide out at inopportune moments. The best iron rakes are *bow rakes*. The two ends of the tined working bar are bent back into a bow, welded together at the tips, and inserted into a slot in the end of the handle. The very best types have the bow welded to a sturdy metal socket that encloses the tip of the handle. Leaf rakes are of little use in a food garden. My favorite leaf rake is expandable and made of aluminum.

SMART *Gardener*

Before each gardening season begins, draw a plan of your garden with the planting beds and aisles sketched in. On the plot plan, enter the kinds of vegetables you want to grow and approximately when you plan to plant them. An 11x17-inch tablet of graph paper using four boxes to the inch will be a big help.

Kneeling Bench

I couldn't do without mine. It saves my back and knees when I have delicate weeding tasks or when I am picking strawberries or bush beans. The handles at the ends of the bench help me when I need to stand up. When I am setting out plants, I flip my bench over and kneel on the cushioned lower surface of the seat. When I have to get up, the U-shaped legs give me leverage that spares my knees. I try to avoid kneeling without the bench because I have to get my feet directly under my body to straighten up. I'm not complaining, not as long as I can get up from the contorted positions required for gardening.

A bow rake is a useful tool for preparing beds for planting.

Small Stuff

I have more trowels, stout garden knives, pruning shears (secateurs, technically speaking), bulb planters, and dandelion diggers than I will ever use. I have a quick-release belt with pockets for small stuff but I rarely wear it. I suppose I am just an old-fashioned gardener. Oddly, one of my most useful tools is an inexpensive bread knife with a long, thin, flexible blade with a serrated edge. I find it useful when I need to remove pot-bound plants. I can slide it down around the root ball and saw up and down to cut the roots that are clinging to the inside wall of the pot. The chrome-plated blade never rusts and the sturdy plastic handle has held up to several years of sun, rain, and soil.

Stakes and a Maul

I keep a supply of 30-inch pine surveyor's stakes handy, along with a hard-rubber maul designed for bumping dents out of autos. The maul has a waterproof handle; its head won't rust like an iron sledgehammer. I use the stakes at the corners of vegetable beds as hose guards and as temporary row-end markers when I am stretching twine to mark straight rows. I have two short-handled, iron sledgehammers as well, but when driving in metal fence posts, I prefer my tubular metal post driver with an enamel finish. It makes that hard job easy, and is kind to my fragile old hands.

BUY THE BASICS, *Improvise the Rest*

WHEN I SEE AN ANNOUNCEMENT proudly introducing a new garden tool, I never know whether to laugh or to cry. **Most seem to be designed to make money rather than to fulfill a real need.** Some are so ridiculous or impractical that I end up smacking my forehead with my palm and shouting something unprintable. I wouldn't dare risk laying one down in the garden because if I fell on it, I might not be able to fish out my cell phone and call 911. A few inventions are so complicated that I call them "hardware stores on a stick." The metal benders just keep on trying. — *Walter Chandoha*

Your hands are often the most useful tool of all.

Wheelbarrows and Carts

There is always something to be hauled in or out of a garden. A wheelbarrow is the logical choice for most gardeners. The conventional single-wheeled variety is okay for most uses, but when fully loaded, it requires some "driving" skill—they tend to tip over and dump the load. A two-wheeled cart is somewhat more maneuverable and almost untippable. Some of these are low-slung with a body made of heavy plastic; others have a three-sided wooden body riding on big bicycle wheels. Still another option, a child's wagon. I've used one of these for hauling harvests from the garden to the house or schlepping a 40-pound bag of fertilizer from the car to the garden.

An upturned wheelbarrow (left) and a two-wheeled cart await their next gardening assignments.

A toy wagon makes an excellent substitute for a wheelbarrow.

The Three "E"s: Ease, Economy & Enjoyment

Because you are reading this book, it's likely that you want to save some money by growing your own food. But you just aren't able to devote every waking minute to the task. It would also be nice if the hours you did spend in your garden were enjoyable and rewarding. Judging by the recent increase in vegetable seed and plant sales, you are not alone.

While there are no concrete statistics on gardeners like yourself, it's reasonable to assume that you are part of a group that is willing to invest the "sweat equity" required for preparing the soil, planting, weeding, and harvesting.

The folks who need to stretch their incomes a bit further to meet expenses are part of a demographic group that I suspect is becoming more involved in food gardening. They are still young enough to manage good-sized gardens, and have the time and enthusiasm to experiment with new ways to prepare and preserve their home-grown produce. Some may even grow enough vegetables and fruit to donate to a local food bank. I continue to hope that more young families will join in such endeavors, although I understand their time constraints.

In addition to the practical aspects, other reasons for planting a food garden include the emotional, psychological, and health benefits. The satisfaction of providing for your family, friends, and community is a powerful reason, but equally gratifying is the knowledge that the food you produce is free of contaminants and tastes a whole lot better than shipped-in produce.

Of course, you can value your food garden solely on a cost-benefit ratio. If and when you do compare the cost of purchasing produce versus producing your own, you should factor in the cost of your many trips to and from the grocery store. After all, your personal time has value, too, and having home-canned or frozen vegetables and fruit in your pantry is a valuable time and money saver. Once your food garden expands to 500 square feet or more, and you learn how to orchestrate interplanting and succession planting, you can confidently expect to save money on the produce you grow.

Make Gardening Easy

Minimize Weeds from the Get-Go

Your first year of gardening can determine how much time you will spend weeding over the next several years. You need to start by eliminating as many weed and grass seeds and roots of perennial grasses as possible. If you also modify your soil with an organic soil conditioner, you will help to minimize weeds and sprouting grasses for several years. The few that do germinate or sprout can be hoed or pulled out of the crumbly soil with little difficulty.

On the other hand, if you merely dig up the soil, sod and all, and throw in some seeds, you will encourage grass clumps and the sprouting of weed seeds that have been lying dormant for many years. This will make it extremely difficult to thin out crops of vegetables that produce small, slow-growing seedlings because these will be hard to distinguish from the weedlings.

For many years, the commonly accepted method for reducing aggressive perennial grasses and weeds was to spray with a glyphosate weed and grass killer. Now, because research is throwing doubt on the safety of many herbicides, organic gardeners opt instead to remove the top 2 inches of soil or turf where weed seeds and perennial roots are concentrated. Fortunately, you will find many uses for this extra soil, such as filling low spots.

Another way to deal with weeds is to cover the worked-up soil with a sheet of plastic anchored around the edges. This is touted as a way to sterilize soil, thus killing weed seeds and roots. The problem is that the heat that collects beneath the plastic tends to rise and move to the top of the slope, leaving the lower areas of the garden without its benefits.

The beet garden pictured here shows the dramatic difference between a food plot where weeds have not been managed (above), and the same garden after extensive weeding (below).

HOW TO USE
"Top-Kill" Herbicide

IF YOU DECIDE TO USE A "TOP-KILL" HERBICIDE, **it won't kill the roots of perennial grasses and broadleaf weeds, but it will make the above-ground parts of these plants decompose faster when turned under.** Here is how to do this:

- After waiting the recommended time for sprayed weeds to die, run a tiller over the ground or **turn under the dead vegetation using a spade.**
- Next, irrigate the soil with a sprinkler for about an hour.
- Wait three weeks for more weeds to sprout; then **add soil conditioner and fertilizer**, and mix them into the top 6 inches of soil.
- Rake the garden more or less level; then shovel soil from the aisles onto the beds to raise their level. **Discard stones and sticks and sticky lumps of clay**, and of course, the roots of perennial grasses and broadleaf weeds.
- Check that aisles have sufficient slope for drainage, and then **spread mulch in the aisles.**

Lettuce and corn mulched with black plastic grow weed free.

IF YOU CHOOSE NOT to use a herbicide to control weeds:

- **Use a spade to remove the top 2 inches of soil or sod.**
- **Till or spade the scalped soil to "spade depth"** (8 to 9 inches deep).
- Irrigate the soil and wait three weeks for weed seeds or perennial roots to sprout.
- Rake the garden more or less level, watching for and removing fleshy roots of perennial grasses and weeds. Discard stones and sticks.
- **Spread soil conditioner and fertilizer,** and work them into the top 6 inches of soil. Wait for three weeks. Rake the soil more or less level.
- Shovel soil from the aisles onto the beds to raise their level. Smooth and level the beds using an iron rake. This will eliminate many of the weed seedlings.
- **Check the aisles for sufficient slope, and spread mulch over walkways.**
- Begin planting your crops.
- If you did not spray with herbicide, you will need to watch for sprigs of Bermuda grass and other perennial weeds, and dig them out promptly. **Simply pulling them out will usually leave enough roots to re-sprout.**

A rather messy-looking alternative, covering tilled soil with used carpet for about a month during warm weather, will help reduce the weed population.

By the way, I prefer to spade soil rather than to pulverize it with a power tiller. I need the exercise, and spading doesn't aggravate any energy crisis other than my own. My partner and I keep three spades in our tool racks, all long-handled, round-pointed, and sharpened. One is lightweight with a standard-size blade, another has a small or "lady's" blade for setting out perennials. The third spade has a steel handle and a heavy-duty blade. I use it for prying out rocks and stumps. For more information on gardening tools, see Chapter 4, beginning on page 56.

Never Let Weeds Get Out of Hand

You will have to deal with some weeds throughout every growing season. They will sprout from seeds that blow in on the wind or that lurk in the soil. The trick is to dig weedlings out of beds and aisles before they go to seed or spread a network of perennial roots. But keep in mind that every time you disturb the soil, you expose a few more dormant weed seeds. Take a dandelion digger with you on your weed safaris. With its small, V-pointed, long-shank blade you can cut roots deep in the soil and pull the weed out with little disturbance. Throw weeds into your compost pile. If you leave them where they were pulled, they may take root and regrow. You will discover that the day following a rain or a deep irrigation is ideal for weeding.

If you pull, dig out, or hoe weeds as soon as you see them, and don't allow them to go to seed, you will soon reduce the number that sprout in your garden. While I will agree academically that weeds among your vegetables might attract beneficial insects, I have to point out that weeds compete strongly with vegetables for plant nutrients and soil moisture.

Rid your garden of weeds when they are still small.

PLANTS THAT *Act Like Weeds*

TRUST ME: YOU ARE ASKING FOR TROUBLE if you grow any flavor of mint or any species of fennel or garlic chives in your garden soil. I've been there and done that, and I am still fighting **spearmint and bronze fennel** sprouting from roots and seeds. I made the mistake of neglecting a mint plant that was growing in a half barrel in an out-of-the-way corner. I couldn't see that it was flowering and setting seeds. Years later, mint sprouts continue to pop up here and there.

Fennel is such a robust, free-seeding plant that it has been declared an invasive weed in some states. Garlic chives are just as determined and will persist as a weed for years after you dig out and discard the original plants. I can remember an extension agent from Texas (let's not mention the county) who confessed to "introducing more weeds to his part of Texas than any other human being." He prefaced this by saying that he was and still is interested in new kinds of plants and many times has ordered seeds of species as soon as they were offered in catalogs. Many new ornamental introductions apparently like the hot, humid summers and relatively mild winters in his climate, and reproduce as fast as fire ants.

Robust plants such as mint can act like invasive weeds, popping up for years in your garden soil. The best defense is to keep these plants contained in pots or half-barrels.

I'M STILL TRYING TO RATIONALIZE my lifelong practice of working up vegetable beds each fall with the **emerging information on the advantages of not tilling garden soil.** Beginning with this writing, I will dress sifted compost or stable litter atop vegetable beds when fall brings cool weather and will work furrows into it for planting seeds and setting out started plants. Because I don't bother with hot composting, a few weed seeds will sprout atop my vegetable beds. **It's a fair tradeoff for preserving the ecosystem beneath the surface of my garden.** For a more in-depth discussion, see Chapter 9, "Advances in Organic Gardening," beginning on page 164.

Regular Picking and Grooming

It makes good sense to harvest crops as soon as they are ready. Doing so prolongs the picking season and reduces the stress on plants. Fruits that drop on the ground should either be salvaged or put in the compost pile, as should chopped prunings.

The degree of grooming depends on how visible your garden is from windows in the house or from the street, how much free time you have, and whether you are a fastidious person by nature. Routine, periodic grooming takes less time than playing catch-up with a weed crop that has gotten out of hand.

You can enjoy a prolonged picking season of vegetables such as sweet corn by staggering plantings weeks apart.

Vegetables in Containers

Vegetables with large frames are not suitable for container growing. Even the compact varieties of summer squash will flop over the rims and demand frequent watering. Bush beans, peas, and corn are impractical because you can't harvest enough from a single container to make a meal. Pole beans attached to tall stakes and lashed together at the top with twine might give you enough pods for a meal for two from a single picking.

Herbs, strawberries, and small, quick-growing vegetables, such as leaf lettuce, onions from sets, and spinach, all grow well in containers. Swiss chard, in as many colors as Joseph's coat, puts on a spectacular show all summer. In the South and warm West, give chard afternoon shade to maintain moisture.

Keeping Aisles and Beds Neat

I'm not a neat freak, but I am pragmatic about keeping one's mate happy. Mine happens to be a garden designer with a sharp eye for color, symmetry, and finish in landscapes, including food gardens. "If Momma ain't happy, ain't nobody happy" is my garden mantra, so I keep my aisles neat with hardwood bark mulch.

Swiss chard's colorful stems make a spectacular display in containers.

SMART *Gardener*

Keep a journal. Even expert gardeners make mistakes. Keeping a journal helps you avoid repeating mistakes and continually sharpens your mastery of soil management, succession planting, and interplanting. You can keep your journal in a loose-leaf notebook or, if you are a computer whiz, as a spreadsheet. Keeping a journal is especially important if you are an organic gardener because you will need to make notes on the effectiveness of biological controls you used against pests. Most of all, a journal will remind you of the varieties or hybrids that grew well.

Direct-seeded lettuce is spaced in neat, clean rows.

Make It Economical

Bulk Is Better

Recently, I heard a local radio announcer describe how to obtain municipal compost in bulk. My town, Columbia, Missouri, has had more than its share of windstorms. Also, crews are always removing trees near power lines before a winter storm does the job for them. This produces an abundance of green wood and foliage, which is put through a barrel grinder and composted until it turns black and takes on a pleasant, fertile odor.

Interestingly, the announcer said, "orders for 100 cubic yards or more must be reserved in advance." Apparently, commercial landscapers are utilizing this economical source of organic matter. If you need to load the compost into a pickup truck, municipal employees will help you using a tractor-mounted front end loader.

Gardeners with SUVs or vans can bring garbage cans and pitchforks and take home as much as their vehicle can carry, at no cost. Compost is heavy, and some gardeners have had to dump a can or two to operate their vehicle safely. By the way, I mentioned using a pitchfork. Shovels don't work well with compost because of its coarse texture. When you buy a pitchfork, get one with as many tines as possible. Farmers call these models "manure forks," and they are well worth the extra cost. They are intended for moving chunky materials that tend to fall between the tines of standard pitchforks. See Chapter 4, beginning on page 56, for more information on gardening tools.

Many municipal sanitation dumps provide a separate area for leaf compost, which is free for the taking (below).

Save Money on Seeds

Consider ordering large packets of seeds and sharing them with friends. Certain catalogs offer king-size "trade packets" and small-bulk quantities. While intended primarily for small-scale commercial growers, groups can buy seeds in large increments and share them among members. Also, become adept at direct seeding of fast-growing crops rather than starting them from purchased plants.

Seeds of hybrid vegetables may cost twice as much or more than seeds of open-pollinated varieties. For this reason, you should plant conservatively and store any leftover seeds in your refrigerator for later planting.

To store leftover vegetable and flower seed, fold over the top of the packet, close it securely with tape, and place it in a freezer bag. Don't put seeds in the freezer;

One way to save money on seeds and seedlings is to buy them in bulk and split the cost with other gardeners.

they will survive better in the general-storage section of your fridge. Write the month and year of storage on the tape used for sealing the packet.

Home-Built Hose Guards

You may need to pull water hoses through your food garden, and hoses tend to knock over plants, especially those at the corners of beds. Even though they aren't pretty, I hammer 30-inch pine contractors' stakes into the corner of my beds. About 2 feet of stake sticks up above the ground, enough to shunt hoses to the side to prevent the hoses from ruining my plants. You can buy plastic hose guards that rotate as hoses rub against them. They work, but I would need so many in my garden that they would break the bank.

Maintain Raised Beds without Framing

For a long time, I would not use treated wood in my food garden. I could not believe that wood that was pressure treated with chromated copper arsenate could be safe around food crops. Apparently other people agreed, including parents concerned about its use in playgrounds. The wood industry has since switched to a copper-based preservative that contains neither chromium nor arsenic. I know that redwood and bald cypress timbers and logs of eastern red cedar and black locust are naturally resistant to termites and rot, but I'd rather save the money and spend it on seeds, plants, and soil conditioners in lieu of expensive framing for beds.

So I spread organic fertilizer every fall season after cleanup. Then I haul soil conditioner from a holding pile to the garden, dress it 2 or 3 inches deep over existing beds, shovel soil that has washed into aisles back into the beds, and rake the beds into the desired shape. The yearly applications of soil conditioner are gradually raising the level of soil in my beds to 2 or 3 inches above

the level of the aisles. There is no longer a need to spade my beds; an abundant crop of earthworms does the job for me.

This intensive approach is fine for a small garden such as mine, but a different and somewhat rougher-looking approach is often used in southern gardens with slow-draining, heavy clay soil. There, soil is shoveled or plowed to form high, narrow beds for planting crops like sweet potatoes and okra, and the aisles, or "middlings," are made wide enough to accommodate a wheeled cultivator. Were I still gardening there, I would choose to cover the aisles with 2 to 3 inches of straw. During some years, straw won't stay put. Extremely heavy rains, locally dubbed "toad stranglers" or "trash movers," often visit the South. Driving the occasional stake through straw mulch to pin it to the ground helps to keep it from washing down to the low end of the aisle. The stakes can be removed after the first heavy rain.

These raised beds that were prepared in the fall are now ready for spring planting.

Tiny Tim tomatoes grown in cast-iron pots.

Make Your Own Potting Soil

Garden soil is seldom suitable for containers. Containers need near-perfect drainage, and ordinary garden soil is too dense to provide it. Garden soil shrinks from the sides of containers when dry, which makes watering difficult. Good-grade potting soils are formulated specifically for use in containers. The most expensive include controlled-release fertilizer and an absorbent material that prolongs intervals between irrigations. Cheap, dense potting soil is as bad or worse than garden soil and may be loaded with weed seeds.

Don't try to improve drainage in garden soil or potting soil by adding sand. It will clog pores in the soil and impede, not improve, drainage. For very windy gardens, filling the bottom quarter of a container with coarse sand or pea gravel will add enough weight to lessen the chance of its blowing over. Gardeners are often tempted to half-fill large containers with lightweight junk such as squashed cold-drink cans, plastic peanuts, or straw. I advise against it because plants would grow better in containers filled top to bottom with potting soil.

You can make a pretty good potting soil by mixing one part premoistened sphagnum peat moss with two parts of shredded, composted hardwood bark. Blend in an ounce or two of pelletized dolomitic limestone per gallon of mix to supply calcium and magnesium and to adjust the soil pH to the level preferred by plants. Add your choice of organic or controlled-release fertilizer, following the directions on the package. Mix it all together in a wheelbarrow or tub. Use promptly.

INSALATA CAPRESE Á LA CHANDOHA

Like my late wife Maria, my daughter, also Maria, is a traditionalist—especially when it comes to Italian food. Even more so with salads. We've had a friendly ongoing dispute on how to make *insalata caprese*—the classic Italian tomato and mozzarella salad.

Like her mother, she keeps it simple and traditional—a dusting of salt and pepper over the sliced tomatoes and mozzarella, a sprinkle of chopped basil, and a drizzle of extra-virgin olive oil. She tells me this is the way it is served in Milan, where she photographs the twice-yearly fashion shows.

I agree that the traditional way is OK. However, when I cook, I like to use recipes as a point of departure. I often add something, subtract something, vary quantities, and the like. To the traditional caprese, I may add some minced garlic, a touch of balsamic vinegar, and sometimes some grated Parmesan cheese. Whatever version we make, it is always served with crusty Italian bread to mop up the dressing — *Walter Chandoha*

Make Gardening Enjoyable

Take Classes

If you're serious about ramping up your gardening know-how and can commit to "giving back" some of what you've learned to your community, think about signing up for a Master Gardening Course. Extension specialists teach these classes, and they are often held in the evenings at county Extension offices. A charge is assessed, mostly to cover the comprehensive manuals on gardening in local climate and soil conditions. The curriculum usually consists of 50 hours of classroom time and takes you through all facets of flower and vegetable gardening and lawn care.

When you are accepted into a class, it is with the understanding that you will volunteer for a minimum of 50 hours of service to other gardeners. This pledge can be fulfilled by fielding questions on a local gardening "hot line," staffing a booth at a garden show, or helping to grow food for the needy, all of which are designed to reinforce what you have been taught about gardening. There are approximately 80,000 Master Gardeners in North America, with skills that range from adequate to expert. Gardening expertise is based in part on years of experience, but the course gives you a solid foundation on which to build.

Visit Your Nearest Botanical Garden

Most states have at least one botanical garden of note. Often, these were private estates that were endowed to foundations that have transformed them into destinations for horticultural displays and education. Every

Many state universities offer evening classes and extensive literature on regional agriculture and gardening.

major botanical garden offers classes and exhibitions on different specialties of gardening. Nothing can compare with a well-grown and clearly labeled food garden for bringing lessons to life. Certain botanical gardens are renowned for the many bulletins they publish on various areas of gardening. The Brooklyn Botanic Gardens in New York City is a leading example.

Because of their size and complexity, botanical gardens can be a bit overwhelming to the beginning gardener. If possible, plan to visit several times throughout the year to take in seasonal displays and to chat with staff members. Gradually, you will come to appreciate the visual and intellectual feast provided for you. Admission tickets are reasonably priced when you consider the cost of staffing and maintaining a huge garden in pristine condition.

Add Structures for Gardening Pleasure

How gratifying it is when you can sit and revel in the beauty of your garden without worrying about weeding or watering. I derive great satisfaction from gazing at the high fence of weathered grape stakes that surrounds my food plot, as well as the graceful arch over the entrance, designed by my life partner and given to me as an 80th birthday present. I get a good feeling, too, from the rus-

---

SMART *Gardener*

Bulletins on the many aspects of gardening are expensive to print and distribute. Colleges of Agriculture and Horticulture everywhere are converting their printed bulletins into databases that can be accessed by home gardeners and commercial growers. Some states employ webmasters who, if they don't know the answers to questions that arrive via the Internet, know where to find answers. There may be a modest charge for subscribing to monthly summaries of new or revised publications and seasonal reminders of what to plant, and when. You can review the summaries and follow links to areas of special interest to you.

Chimney flues elevate herbs for easier picking.

tic arbors I have rigged for pole beans. I scrounged and trimmed stout saplings from trash-tree species in our woods to make the poles, and lashed them together with twine. The arbor resembles an inverted "V," held together with poles laid across the top. I usually work alone in my garden, but holding up that house of cards long enough to tie it together made me wish my partner were nearby to lend a hand.

I have also altered my habit of growing tomatoes in tall cages. I have found that cages are visually overbearing and have returned to 5-foot posts for support. However, the most beautiful structure I've ever employed was a long line of native brush cut to match the height of the fence, planted with high-climbing, super-fragrant

'Cupani Original' sweet-pea vines. Yes, I do occasionally steal space in my food garden for ornamental flowers.

On visits to public food gardens I have seen some highly imaginative structures, including twig gates, tripods, obelisks, sundials, and gazing balls. In the desert Southwest I have seen high ramadas—open shelters with roofs made of wood laths nailed over crosspieces. The sturdy laths were spaced far enough apart to create about 40 percent shade. The shade helped to keep the soil temperature a few degrees cooler, and I could see the difference in the improved growth of leafy vegetables that were protected from the blazing sun. All of these structures served as conversation pieces and added visual interest to the gardens.

Use Containers as Beauty Spots

During recent years, I have depended more and more on large containers to provide visual emphasis as well as to increase production. Containers placed singly or in groups can lift your garden out of the ordinary while producing lots of flowers or produce. When in groups, they display better if some are elevated on blocks. Plants in containers need more frequent watering than those in the ground—as often as daily during hot, dry, windy weather. Large containers, 15 to 30 gallons in capacity, always produce better results than small pots. I use oak half-barrels. They are good for three seasons of use if raised off the ground with bricks. In Zone 9 and south, large, fired clay, concrete, fiberglass, or glazed containers can remain in the garden year round. They hold up better than wood containers.

Containers are a summertime delight in hardiness Zone 7 and north, and a year-round delight in warmer climates. Enjoy their beauty and bounty, but in northern climes, make sure to empty and store containers away for the winter. Freezing and thawing can ruin half-barrels and can crack fired clay pots. Before hard freezes come in the fall, transplant perennial herbs from containers into the garden and mulch them. Plants in containers are far more likely to die from winter cold and drought than those growing in the garden.

Flowers Among Your Food Crops

A row of mixed flowers grown for cutting looks natural in a food garden and is bound to delight children and to earn Brownie points. Sunflowers, which have a place in flower gardens, are a poor choice for food gardens. Birds scatter sunflower seeds that volunteer all over the place the following year. Sunflower plants are somewhat *allelopathic*, which means that their roots produce a substance that discourages the growth of nearby plants.

Benches in Food Gardens

We have two ancient teak benches in our ornamental garden. Over the years, weathering has turned them gray and has garnished them with lichens. I sit on them occasionally, but not for long. Despite their utility, they are more like garden art than functional outdoor furniture. At my age, I really need to sit more often, but I don't have a fixed bench in my food garden. It would just take up space that I would rather devote to a food crop. So I keep my little folding garden bench handy for whenever I feel that my git-up-and-go has got up and gone. My portable bench isn't garden art, but it takes the load off!

Beautiful to see. Wonderful to eat.

Now the Day is Over...

I can remember an old hymn from my childhood. It began, "Now the day is over, night is drawing nigh. Shadows of the evening, steal across the sky." It could be a metaphor for my life, I suppose, but I prefer to relate it to the fall season of gardening.

At this writing, frost has killed all my warm-season vegetables. A hard freeze is predicted for tonight, and will probably finish off a row of Swiss chard. With a little luck, a row of spinach could survive for a few weeks. I've trimmed my asparagus to the ground and laid aside the ferny tops until the ground freezes. I dressed stable compost over the asparagus bed to give the crowns a good start next spring.

Now, I will wait a month and dress the wilted tops over the bed. Mice should have, by then, found playgrounds elsewhere. Before I put away the wheelbarrow, I will bring a load of mulch from the storage pile and dress it over my row of carrots. Next spring, I will rake the mulch into adjacent aisles. The mulch will delay the freezing of soil, and I can continue digging carrots until late December. My strawberries have been thinned and mulched with stable litter, as have my blueberry bushes.

What else is there to do? I've moved tender succulents inside to carry them through the winter under fluorescent lights. I've unhooked, drained, and put away my garden hoses. I can't think of a single thing left undone in my food garden. Now, I'll just have to wait until the shrubs in our ornamental garden are fully dormant before I get out my hand shears, pruning saw, and loppers and begin trying to improve on Nature. It's a good feeling to have the free time to put on my garden writer's hat and help you to enjoy growing good, healthy food in your own garden.

There's no rule that says you can't grow flowers in your food garden. Their beauty is a feast for the eyes, above and left. When the day's work is done, a garden bench is the perfect spot for enjoying the fruits of your labors with loved ones, below.

Selected Vegetables

Best Methods for Starting Each Kind

Centuries of experience has established the best methods for starting each kind of food crop. For some vegetables and herbs, direct seeding is the only practical option. For others, starting seedlings under indoor lights or buying started plants is more realistic. Only a few vegetables, notably rhubarb and perennial onions, are customarily started from offsets, or "pups." Scallions can be grown from the small onion bulbs called "sets," and potatoes are grown from "seed pieces" cut from sprouting potato tubers.

We will not list the depth to which seeds of each kind need to be covered. As a general rule, cover seeds up to three times their diameter, which translates to a very light scattering of soil over tiny seeds. In heavy clay loam soil, cover small seeds with coarse play sand to reduce the crusting that can impede germination. During hot, dry weather, plant seeds in the bottom of 2-inch deep furrows and lay an old, untreated board over the furrow to reduce evaporation. Check the seed packet for specific recommendations on how far apart plants should be after thinning, and the amount of spacing between rows. **NOTE: The key to the "Essential Stats" that accompany each vegetable, fruit, and herb can be found on page 10.**

Sweet potatoes, like white potatoes, are usually grown from sprouting tubers known as "seed pieces," top. Many vegetables, such as broccoli, grow best when planted as seedlings, left.

COMMON
Pests and Diseases

Most insects, such as this tomato hornworm (above), prefer to infest only one species of vegetable. But some, such as aphids and Japanese beetles, are less particular about what they'll devour. In each listing, we name the insects that are most troublesome to that vegetable or fruit, but you should rely on the Extension Service of your state for specific information on controlling them.

VEGETABLES AND BERRIES ARE VERY ADAPTABLE. They can thrive and produce heavy crops on a wide range of soils, as long as the soil is neither too acid nor alkaline, is well drained, and has a good content of organic matter. But each kind does have an inflexible window of time for planting. Plant too early, and frost or cold soil can cause crop failure. Plant too late, and the combination of summer heat and sun can force leafy vegetables to flower and set seeds, thus interfering with the pollination required for fruit to develop. **These windows of time are bound on one side by the spring frost-free date and on the other by the first killing frost of the fall season.** Refer to Chapter 1, page 22, for detailed information about hardiness zones. You may also see these dates visualized in the maps in the Resource Guide, beginning on page 180.

It would be impractical to list the optimal planting dates for each food crop in every climate zone in North America. Fortunately, the names of the seasons remain the same, even though the dates on which each season arrives vary according to zone. For example:

Digging up and relocating fragile lettuce seedlings.

Early spring. This means whenever the soil in your area has dried out enough to work and plant. **Very cold-hardy kinds can be direct seeded, but transplanting of seedlings should be delayed for two or three weeks to escape late killing frosts.** "Early spring" can range from early February in the Deep South and warm West to mid-May in USDA hardiness Zone 3.

Early summer. There are two time-honored yardsticks for determining when to plant warm-season vegetables. **If you have deciduous oak trees in your area, watch for the first leaves to appear.** Or take off your shoes and walk on the soil. If it feels warm to the soles of your feet, it is time to plant. Hold off for two or three weeks before planting seeds of melons and supersweet hybrid corn, and before setting out plants of tomatoes, peppers, and eggplant. Rushing the season with these can lead to disappointment.

Late summer. The date for this season is determined by counting back from the date of the first killing fall frost in your area. Such a date is useful for planting second crops of warm-season vegetables in the South and low elevations of the West, and for direct-seeding of cool-season crops in time for them to be harvested before a hard freeze elsewhere. In such situations, the "days to maturity" listed on seed packets are not reliable, because they don't take into consideration the short, cool, often wet weather of the fall season. It is prudent to order seeds in the spring for late summer planting because retail store packet seed assortments are usually picked over late in the year.

Early fall. This date is relevant only in the deep South and low elevations of the West and Southwest, when short-day onions are ready to be transplanted and where quick crops of cold-hardy leafy vegetables can be grown for harvest before they are injured by heavy frost. Some of their winters are free of hard frosts until well into late winter, allowing prolonged harvest of frost-hardy, leafy vegetables.

ASIAN VEGETABLES

Most Asian vegetables grown in North America are the green, leafy types such as pe-tsai, bok choy, Napa cabbage, and garland chrysanthemum, used for stir-frying or salads. Seeds of several mustard relatives including mizuna are available from specialty catalogs. Root crops such as the large, white daikon radish are also part of this family.

ESSENTIAL STATS

- **Life span**
  Grown as annuals. Most are cool-season crops.
- **Grow from**
  Direct seeding to mature during cool weather.
- **When to plant**
  Early spring and again in late summer (fall where winters are mild).
- **Days to maturity**
  Expect 30 to 60 days depending on whether planted in spring or fall.
- **Best site**
  Containers, or as quick-growing crops for inter-cropping.

- **Soil preparation**
  Average garden soil will suffice, but water the plants frequently during dry or windy weather. Harvest spring-planted crops prior to the onset of hot weather.
- **How much to plant**
  For fresh use, 15 feet of row will feed two people. Prolong harvest by gathering only the outer leaves, leaving the terminal bud to grow new leaves.
- **Insect, pest, and plant diseases**
  The small, green larvae of the imported cabbage-worm can riddle leaves. Control with Bt (*Bacillus thuringeriensis*) sprays.

ASPARAGUS

Ready for the table in early spring, spears of homegrown asparagus are a delectable change of fare from processed or shipped-in produce. And as difficult as it feels to endure the two years between planting and the first harvest, the pleasure that comes with the first bite of a freshly picked spear more than compensates for the long wait. That pleasure should continue year after year with minimal effort.

 **ESSENTIAL STATS**

▶ **Life span**
Hardy perennial; can live many years. Short-lived where summers are hot and humid.

▶ **Grow from**
"Crowns," which are one-year-old plants grown from seeds. Ask for male plants with inbred disease resistance. Sowing asparagus seeds in your garden will delay harvest for one year more than planting crowns.

▶ **When to plant**
Early spring over most of the country, fall in the Deep South and low elevations of the Southwest and West.

▶ **How much to plant**
At least two-dozen crowns are needed to feed two people. Plant more if spears are to be frozen.

▶ **Best site**
An out-of-the-way corner of the garden where the billowy ferns that grow from the spears won't get in the way.

▶ **Soil preparation**
Dig in lots of organic soil conditioner and dried cattle manure to spade depth. Asparagus crowns resent disturbance and like to remain where originally planted. Male asparagus plants are more productive than female, which are burdened by crops of berries.

▶ **Harvesting**
Don't harvest spears until the third year after planting (fourth for seeds), to give the crowns time to build up the food reserves necessary to support heavy harvests. Allow at least one spear per crown to develop into a fern. Don't cut them off; the ferns are needed to replenish and strengthen the crowns.

▶ **Insect, pest, and plant diseases**
Don't let asparagus beetles get started. You will see their dark larvae feeding on young ferns. Control them with sprays of Neem oil or insecticidal soap before they mature, multiply, and spread.

SMART *Gardener*

Top-dress early vegetables such as asparagus and rhubarb with organic fertilizer in late spring to encourage growth. In late fall, after you trim off the dry ferns of asparagus, spread 2 inches of compost or dried cattle manure over the bed.

BEANS (a.k.a. Green Bean, Snap Bean, Bush Bean)

Green beans come in round or oval-pod varieties and a range of colors. "Bush" varieties should be tall and strong enough so that pods don't sprawl on the ground. "Pole" varieties develop twining tendrils that will climb brush or strings to a height of 5 feet or more. If you enjoy color in your food garden, try planting scarlet runner beans; they are truly ornamental edibles.

ESSENTIAL STATS

▶ **Life span**
Warm-weather annual. Produces three or four pickings of pods then dies, all within 45–90 days.

▶ **Grow from**
Direct seed in garden rows in warm soil. Seeds sprout in five to seven days.

▶ **When to plant**
Early summer, at least one week after the spring frost-free date.

▶ **Best site**
Full sun all day, well-drained soil.

▶ **How much to plant**
If you plan to freeze beans, plan on a 25-foot row to feed two people. Bush beans are often planted in rows 4 inches apart so they can support each other.

▶ **Continuing care**
Other than watering twice weekly during dry spells and watching for insect pests, bush beans and pole beans require little care. Pick beans every four or five days to maintain high production.

▶ **Harvesting**
To avoid breaking the plant, hold the stem in one hand while pulling the pods with the other. Pick pods before they become lumpy with ripening seeds. If some pods are lumpy or turning yellow, shell them and cook the green seeds.

▶ **Insect, pest, and plant diseases**
Rabbit and deer love seedlings, and jays and crows will also pull them up. Protect seedlings with floating row covers, but remove the covers when temperatures exceed 70° F. If Mexican bean beetles appear (recognizable by their orange- and black-stripes and turtle backs), hand pick and drown them. Prevent their reproduction by spraying with a special species of bacillus that targets their larvae but doesn't kill adult beetles. Mosaic virus can also attack beans. Buy varieties with inbred resistance to its various types.

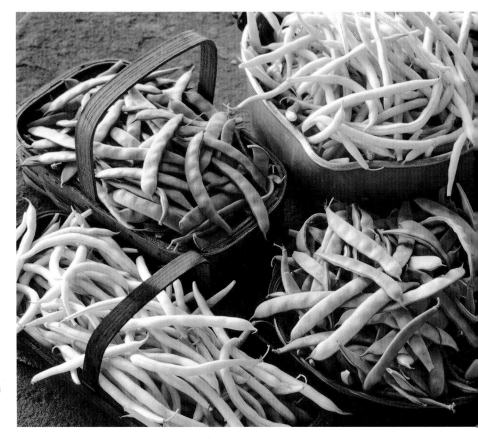

BEANS, LIMA *(a.k.a. Butter Beans)*

Lima bean varieties with thick, fleshy seeds are the most popular. However, in the Deep South, small-seeded varieties are preferred for their resistance to heat and humidity. Some varieties have speckled seeds and a slightly stronger flavor. Pole varieties of butter beans are noted for their productivity over extended periods of hot, humid weather.

ESSENTIAL STATS

▶ **Life span**
Warm weather annual; matures in 70–75 days from planting.

▶ **Grow from**
Direct seed in garden rows in warm soil. Seeds sprout in five to seven days.

▶ **When to plant**
Early summer, two to three weeks after the spring frost-free date.

▶ **Best site**
Full, daylong sun, away from tall plants that could shade them. Well-drained soil is essential; sandy loam produces the best crops.

▶ **How much to plant**
Plan on 20 to 30 feet of row for two people.

▶ **Continuing care**
The time frame for harvesting lima beans is short. You will need to let a few pods become overly mature before the balance develops the plump pods that signal readiness for picking. Don't pick young pods; they will just have to be discarded. The comparative late maturity of the limas exposes them to hotter weather than snap beans, which can adversely affect pollination and pod set.

SMART *Gardener*

It is sheer folly to rely on rain to supply vegetables with the water they need. Gardeners have too much invested in plants, seeds, organic matter, and their own time and labor to give plants less water than is needed for their maximum growth and development. A single faucet can serve a 5,000-square-foot garden, but two are much better. Two faucets with "Y" adapters can handle four hoses, or soaker hoses laid down the center of raised beds.

▶ **Harvesting and shelling pods**
Wait until you see lumps in the pods before picking them. To avoid breaking stems, grasp the plant with one hand when pulling pods. Shelling lima beans, especially the small-seeded butter beans, can be tedious.

▶ **Insect, pest, and plant diseases**
See information for green beans.

BEET

A surprising menu of beet choices awaits you. Roots come not only in the familiar dark purple-red but in golden shades and in round, flattened, and oblong shapes. Certain hybrid varieties have been bred for high sugar content, while others, such as 'Green Top Bunching', were developed to produce both bright red roots and tender chard-like leaves for cooking.

ESSENTIAL STATS

▷ **Life span**
Biennial, grown as an annual. Roots develop best during cool weather. Allow 50 to 75 days for roots to size up.

▷ **Grow from**
Direct seeding with seeds soaked overnight in water spiked with two or three drops of dishpan detergent. Rinse thoroughly and drain. Plant primed seeds promptly. Expect germination in four to ten days. Beet seedlings resent being transplanted unless you move them in clusters with root balls intact.

▷ **When to plant**
Late spring in Zone 6 and north. In the Deep South and warm west, plant seeds from late summer through fall for the best results.

▷ **Best site**
Sunny, well-drained soil, made porous by digging-in generous amounts of fine-textured organic soil conditioner. Sandy loam soil is ideal.

▷ **How much to plant**
Plan on 20 feet of row for two people; double that amount if you plan on pickling a substantial quantity of roots. The Internet will give you detailed instructions on pickling beets.

▷ **Continuing care**
Beets demand rigorous thinning, perhaps two or three times, beginning when the seedlings are quite small. Roots should be 2 to 3 inches apart.

▷ **Harvesting**
Peach-size roots that are free of fiber have the best flavor when canned. This means that spring-planted crops need to be harvested before days grow long, hot, and dry. Fall-planted beets give you more flexibility; the roots remain in good condition longer in cool soil.

▷ **Insect, pest, and plant diseases**
Slugs, brown snails, and earwigs can devour seedlings. As soon as the first sprouts appear, scatter snail bait with iron phosphate as the active ingredient.

BROCCOLI

Broccoli was relatively unknown in the United States until after WWII, when supermarkets began offering frozen foods. Like cauliflower, the immature flower buds and stems of broccoli are edible and packed with vitamins and minerals. Broccoli is a bit more difficult to grow than its close relative cabbage because broccoli is more demanding of cool weather while forming heads.

ESSENTIAL STATS

▷ **Life span**
Although technically a biennial, broccoli is grown as an annual.

▷ **Grow from**
When started from good-sized seedling plants, early varieties or hybrids of broccoli need about 80 days from transplanting to harvest. Direct seeding isn't recommended.

▷ **When to plant**
Early spring in Zone 7 and north. Plants should be hardened off before being transplanted to garden rows, and protected from late frost. Late summer through fall in the Deep South, warm West, and Southwest, to mature during cool weather.

▷ **Best site**
Plant away from the long shadows cast by buildings in early spring. Broccoli needs full sun all day if it is to mature before hot weather. Afternoon shade is helpful to broccoli planted in late summer in hot climates.

▷ **How much to plant**
All the plants in a row of broccoli will mature within one week's time. Therefore, plan to blanch and freeze most of the crop. Because the plants need rather wide spacing, 20 feet of row is needed to feed two people and to provide extra for freezing.

▷ **Continuing care**
Broccoli responds positively to a light mulching to keep the soil moist and cool.

▷ **Harvesting**
Cut the stem on a slant below the central head so water won't soak into the scar and rot the stem. With a little luck, small side heads may form and give you a second harvest.

▷ **Insect, pest, and plant diseases**
Rotate your vegetable crops each year, and use plenty of soil conditioner to prevent infection by diseases that can invade roots. Protect each new transplant from cutworm damage by sinking bottomless food cans into the soil. Control cabbageworms with sprays of Bt bacteria, which are nontoxic to humans and pets.

BRUSSELS SPROUTS

Because they are harvested during the fall and winter, Brussels sprouts are a useful crop for colder areas. After the first frosts, the sprouts hold well on the plants, and they become sweeter. If sprouts are not a favorite, maybe it's because you haven't grown your own—the fresh variety may change your mind.

ESSENTIAL STATS

▶ **Life span**
Biennial, grown as an annual. Needs 100–150 days of relatively cool weather to produce tall stalks that are loaded with rings of tender sprouts.

▶ **Grow from**
Good-sized transplants.

▶ **When to plant**
Not recommended for spring planting except in hardiness Zones 3 and 4 and in coastal regions of the West, where they can also be planted in early fall. Brussels sprouts need extended cool weather to produce good crops.

▶ **Best site**
Good soil at the back of the garden where you won't have to walk around this slow-growing crop to reach others.

▶ **Continuing care**
As sprouts begin to appear you can gradually snip off the lower leaves, leaving only a topknot of foliage. Avoid taking a large percentage of the foliage in one pass, as this can shock the plant. Sprouts need a uniform level of soil moisture during the season and a supplementary side dressing of fertilizer in midseason.

> ### SMART *Gardener*
>
> *To take advantage of newer hybrids, order seeds and start them indoors under fluorescent lights 10 weeks prior to the spring frost-free date. Set seedlings out when they are 8 weeks old.*

▶ **Harvesting**
Sprouts can be snipped off when they are 1 to 2 inches in diameter.

▶ **Insect, pest, and plant diseases**
Cabbageworms are the most common pest. Rotate crops and maintain high levels of organic matter in the soil to prevent damage from root diseases.

CABBAGE

Growing cabbage from well-grown seedlings is easy. You may have a dilemma on your hands at harvest time, though, because all the heads mature at once. Avoid a surplus by planting just a few heads of several varieties or hybrids that mature over an extended period of time.

ESSENTIAL STATS

Life span
Cabbage is a biennial grown in gardens as a cool-weather annual.

Grow from
Started plants. Direct seeding delays maturity until summer, when hot weather can cause the heads to split. Heads mature in 50–75 days from setting out plants.

When to plant
In hardiness Zones 3 through 7, set out well-grown seedlings in early spring. If a hard freeze is predicted, cover the plants with bottomless gallon plastic milk jugs or floating row covers. In the Deep South and low elevation areas of the West and Southwest, late summer plantings fare better. Cool coastal regions of the West and Northwest have more latitude in planting dates for cabbage.

Best site
Early spring plantings can be subjected to heavy rains in April and May. For this reason, raised beds or ridged-up rows are recommended. The extra elevation raises the root zones of plants above cold,

SMART *Gardener*

You can choose between early, mid-season, and main-season cabbage varieties, and between hybrids and open-pollinated varieties. Much of the advantage of hybrid cabbage is in uniform maturity, which isn't all that important to home gardeners.

water-soaked soil at ground level. Avoid planting in the long shadows of buildings in the early spring.

How much to plant
If you grow only one variety or hybrid, not much. Ten feet of row is plenty for two people. You can start seeds indoors under fluorescent lights eight weeks prior to the spring frost-free date. Crops started from seeds in late summer can be transplanted to pots for setting out in the garden.

Continuing care
Cabbage plants require little attention. Just maintain a uniform level of soil moisture, and give the plants a little shot of liquid organic fertilizer if they seem to be lagging.

Harvesting
Using a sharp, flexible knife, cut the stem on a slant so the scar won't hold water. Leave as many basal leaves as possible to support the formation of small side heads.

Insect, pest, and plant diseases
Powdery mildew can become a problem during wet, warm summer weather, but a product called Milstop can be used to control it. Cabbageworms rarely miss an opportunity to riddle the leaves of cabbages, but they can be controlled with sprays of Bt bacteria. Spray as soon as the wrapper leaves begin to arch up to enclose the terminal bud.

CARROT

Carrots can be one of the most gratifying and nutritious crops to grow. In hardiness Zone 5 and north, spring-planted carrots can stay in the ground for months without losing quality. You can grow carrots that are round, tapered, or cylindrical, depending on the variety. Dark colors, such as purple, don't differ in flavor, but new studies indicate they may offer more nutritive value.

ESSENTIAL STATS

Life span
Technically a biennial, but grown as an annual.

Grow from
Direct seeding. Seeds need 10 to 14 days in order to germinate.

When to plant
In early spring and again in late summer through fall, depending on the length of your growing season. To get good germination in dry weather, plant seeds in a 2-inch-deep furrow, cover lightly, soak the row with a sprinkler, and lay a board over the furrow to prevent soil from losing moisture.

Best site
Full sun, in raised beds, made porous by working generous additions of organic amendments into the soil.

How much to plant
A 10- to 15-foot row should give two people plenty of fresh carrots.

Continuing culture
Early and rigorous thinning is required to produce straight, smooth, and unbranched carrot roots. Roots should stand 2 to 3 inches apart. Pulling soil up around the roots in midseason will reduce the incidence of green shoulders on roots.

Harvesting
Water carrots thoroughly before harvesting. Use a long trowel to help pry the roots out of the soil. Attempting to pull roots out by yanking on the tops can result in broken roots.

SMART *Gardener*

You can harvest carrots well into the winter if you mulch with 6 inches of hay that is held down with old boards.

CAULIFLOWER

Cauliflower is a cool-weather vegetable that is closely related to cabbage and broccoli. It requires more attention than its cousins in order to prevent its "curds" from splitting and forming flowers when overly mature or subjected to continued heat. In addition to white, you can find chartreuse, peach, lime green, and violet varieties. A novelty variety called 'Romanesco' develops lime green, cone-shaped pinnacles.

ESSENTIAL STATS

▷ **Life span**
Biennial, grown as an annual. Some varieties mature in as little as 50 days, while others require 75 days.

▷ **Grow from**
Well-grown seedlings. Direct seeding is not recommended.

▷ **When to plant**
Early spring in hardiness Zones 3 through 6. Late summer through fall in the Deep South and West, depending on how long high temperatures persist.

▷ **Best site**
Spring-planted cauliflower has a better chance of forming heads before hot weather if planted in raised beds or ridged-up rows that warm up faster than surrounding soil. Daylong, full sun is required. Where grown for maturity during fall and winter months, afternoon shade can reduce moisture stress on plants.

▷ **How much to plant**
Like broccoli, all your cauliflower plants will mature at nearly the same time. Unless you plan to freeze the excess, 10 feet of row will feed two people. Cauliflower varieties and hybrids come in a range of days to maturity, so planting more than one kind can extend harvest.

▷ **Continuing care**
If you prefer creamy white curds, you will need to blanch the heads. To do this, gather the tips of the long leaves that radiate from the stem when the heads begin to form; then rubber band or tie the leaves together. This forms a canopy over the head, shielding it from much of the sunlight that would turn the heads green or discolor them. Allow a week to go by and re-tie any leaves that may have slipped out.

▷ **Harvesting**
To extend the harvest season, take some of the heads before they are fully mature. Undo the ties to get access to the heads using a sharp, flexible knife.

▷ **Insect, pest, and plant diseases**
Cauliflower attracts the same pests as cabbage but is more sensitive to hot weather, particularly when humidity is high.

CHAYOTE *(a.k.a. Christophine, Chocho, Vegetable Pear, Mango Squash)*

Interest in chayote has grown along with the emigration of people from Mexico, Central America, and the Caribbean to North America. Chayote grows long vines with rather small, cucumber-like leaves and bears pear-shaped fruits that can vary in weight from ½ to 6 pounds. Centuries of selection by families have produced many variations in skin texture and flavor.

ESSENTIAL STATS

▶ **Life span**
Frost-tender perennial, grown as an annual in hardiness Zones 7 and 8. It won't mature fruit further north unless you overwinter plants in a greenhouse and set them out in early summer.

▶ **Grow from**
Purchase a mature chayote fruit, and start it indoors under lights. Lay the fruit on its side or with the stem-end slanted up in potting soil, and provide bottom heat of 70° F or higher. Within two or three weeks, the fruit will split and a sprout will emerge from the single, avocado-like seed.

▶ **When to plant**
Indoors, 10 weeks prior to the spring frost-free date. Transplant to the garden or to a large container two weeks after the spring frost-free date.

▶ **Best site**
Against a west or south-facing wall that will reflect afternoon heat into the plant. Provide a sturdy trellis to support the rampant vines and heavy fruit.

▶ **How much to plant**
A single vine can produce a dozen pear-sized fruit or perhaps six fruits of large-fruited variety. The fruits will retain flavor and texture for a week or two after optimal harvest time.

▶ **Continuing care**
Chayote plants will get by with little care. However, a midsummer mulch of dried cattle manure followed by a good soaking from a sprinkler should produce a flush of blossoms and fruit.

▶ **Harvesting**
Snip off the fruit using pruning shears. Don't try to pull them off, or you can break the vines.

▶ **Insect, pest, and plant diseases**
Chayote has long been grown in Florida, Southern California, and at low elevations in Arizona. In those areas, the plants live over winter, sustained by tuberous roots. In all probability, insects and diseases have discovered those chayote plantings. Farther north, however, home gardeners might have few or no problems with chayote.

SMART *Gardener*

Growing celery. *Because it requires special care and a very long, cool growing season, celery is seldom grown in home gardens. You can start seeds indoors ten weeks before transplanting in mid-spring in the north or in late summer where winters are mild. Allow at least 100 days from planting to harvest.*

COLLARD GREENS

I have to curb my enthusiasm when praising collards. Despite their good taste and nutritive value, not everyone is interested in cooking and eating greens. But I owe a debt to collards; they helped my family to stay healthy during the depths of the Great Depression. Basically a non-heading variant of cabbage, collards are extremely cold tolerant.

ESSENTIAL STATS

▶ **Life span**
Biennial, grown as a cool-weather annual. Collard seeds sprout quickly and within 80 days will produce the first of many meals.

▶ **Grow from**
Direct seeding.

▶ **When to plant**
In Zones 3 through 5 sow seeds in spring as soon as the soil is dry enough to work. Hot weather will damage plants, so harvest them and plant seeds again in late summer for a fall harvest. Farther south, wait until August 15 or later before direct seeding. Sow seeds 3 to 6 inches apart to reduce the chore of thinning.

▶ **Best site**
Collards are not wimpy vegetables; they will thrive wherever planted, if you start them within the window of planting time for your hardiness zone. In the Deep South and warm western areas, afternoon shade will help collards sail through the last days of hot weather before entering the cool, moist days of fall and early winter.

▶ **How much to plant**
Southerners rely so much on collards that it is not unusual to see a 30-foot row planted to provide for two people—12 to 15 collard plants would fit into a row of that length, if the plants were staggered. Collard leaves will "hold" on the plant for weeks after reaching full size, retaining flavor and tenderness.

▶ **Continuing care**
Not much attention is required, just thinning and frequent enough watering to avoid serious wilting. Avoid fertilizing fall-planted collards after the first light frost. The nitrogen fraction could make the plants susceptible to freezing.

▶ **Harvesting**
Nip off the lower leaves a few at a time to avoid shocking the plants. The upper leaves will continue to extract energy from the sun. After several weeks, collards typically show a foot or so of bare central stem, but they keep on ticking. Leaves harvested during hot weather should be placed in a plastic bag and stored in the vegetable keeper. After a week or two, they will be sweeter when cooked.

▶ **Insect, pest, and plant diseases**
Collards are susceptible to the same diseases and insects as cabbages. Cabbageworm infestations can be particularly bad during the waning warm days of late summer. Keep Bt bacteria sprays handy.

CORN, SWEET

There is simply no competition between the corn of yesteryear and the modern hybrids available today. Seed breeders have worked miracles on the native American plant that once had small ears and flavor that was nothing to brag about. Trust me; you don't want to go back to those. Now, sweet corn comes in yellow, white, and bicolor kernels on large ears with a high sugar content that will hold for days.

ESSENTIAL STATS  -

▶ **Life span**
Sweet corn is an annual that can be harvested in 65–80 days.

▶ **Grow from**
Direct seeding, 4 to 6 inches apart in rows 30– 48 inches apart, depending on the hybrid, or in clusters of three or four seeds in a raised hill. Seeds will germinate in five to seven days in warm soil. Pollination is improved if sweet corn is planted in blocks rather than in rows. No pollination, no kernels!

▶ **When to plant**
After spring frost danger, preferably during a warm spell. For extended harvest, make multiple plantings two to three weeks apart.

▶ **How much to plant**
Sweet corn takes up a lot of space for a considerable time, and isn't a good candidate for containers or small gardens. A minimum-size block (a square or rectangular patch of several short rows) for two people would measure 10 feet on the side.

▶ **Continuing care**
When plants are knee-high, dribble corn fertilizer down the furrow, and cut it into the soil 6 to 8 inches away from the stalks. Cover the fertilizer with soil to get more bang for your fertilizer buck.

> ### SMART *Gardener*
>
> *Standard sweet corn hybrids have been around since the early 1930s, and were pretty good for their time. Then, seed breeders produced what are called "Supersweet" hybrids. Most recently, breeders have introduced hybrids which have very tender kernels and a creamy texture.*

▶ **Harvesting**
Check for readiness by splitting the husks at the tip of an ear. Tip kernels should be plump but not beginning to dimple. The silk should be browning at harvest stage. Grasp the stalk above the ear and "snap" the ear off by twisting while pulling down.

▶ **Insect, pest, and plant diseases**
Stewart's wilt, a disease transmitted by the feeding of flea beetles, is most troublesome in areas where the beetles are not killed by sub-zero temperatures. Its symptoms include yellow stripes in the leaves. Corn earworms are a universal problem but can be controlled by spraying a 50:50 mixture of mineral oil and hydrogen peroxide on the silks. The timing of spraying is critical, so ask your Extension Service for details. If you can't contact them, shake the corn tassels atop the plant daily. When you see yellow pollen flying, wait three days before spraying.

CUCUMBER

Apart from a little Vitamin C, cucumbers don't offer much nutritional value. However, pickles and salads just wouldn't be the same without these crunchy vegetables. Cucumbers can be rampant vining plants, so grow them on trellises, or try modern bush varieties such as 'Bush Champion', 'Salad Bush', or 'Fanfare', which are small enough for potting in a container.

ESSENTIAL STATS

Best site
Very well-drained soil. Plant in raised beds filled with highly organic soil. Full sun is imperative, and so is room to ramble. The long vines can be run up trellises or on wire stretched between posts.

How much to plant
Cucumbers will give you an abundance of fruit from several pickings, provided that they get good pollination. Six vines will feed two people.

Continuing care
Vines commonly bloom for a few days before fruit begins to set. The first blossoms are usually all male. A week to 10 days later, the female blossoms form. The females have a swollen stem just behind the blossom. If no baby fruit form for more than a week, try transferring pollen from male blooms to female stigmas using a camel's-hair brush.

Harvesting
Begin harvesting when the first fruits are only half-mature. Don't let fruits stay on the vines past full maturity, or they will drain the plant's vigor.

Insect, pest, and plant diseases
Cucumber beetles are destructive pests that have to be exterminated early and regularly to prevent them from infecting vines. Consult your state Extension Service Web site for insect control recommendations. Use food-can barriers to protect seedlings from cutworm damage.

Life span
Cucumbers are warm-weather annuals.

Grow from
Direct seeding in ridged-up rows or hills. In far northern areas, build raised beds and cover them with black plastic sheeting. Start seeds in pots indoors seven to eight weeks prior to the frost-free date, and transplant them through holes cut in the plastic.

When to plant
In warm soil, 10 to 14 days after the spring frost-free date. Cucumber seeds will rot in cold, wet soil. In the Deep South and low elevations of the West, second crops are possible from direct seeding in late summer.

SMART *Gardener*

In addition to the classes of cucumbers mentioned, you can also buy seeds of heirloom types that may have odd shapes or unusual colors. More importantly, you should look for listings of disease, insect, and soil-organism tolerance.

EGGPLANT

The popularity of eggplant has grown with the practice of grilling vegetables. Seed breeders have responded by developing hybrids with tender skins that don't need to be peeled prior to grilling. The interest in the many ethnic recipes using eggplant has also boosted its appeal. Eggplants have tall, rather leggy plants with leaves as rough as sandpaper.

ESSENTIAL STATS

▸ **Life span**
Definitely a warm-weather annual except in hardiness Zone 10 where plants can live through mild winters. Days to maturity range from 60–80 days from setting out well-grown seedling plants, depending not only on the variety or hybrid but also on prevailing day and night temperatures.

▸ **Grow from**
Transplants started 10 weeks prior to the frost-free date. Seeds sprout best with bottom heat kept at 75–85° F. Move seeded pans to a slightly cooler area when the first sprouts appear.

▸ **When to plant**
Set transplants into warm garden soil two to three weeks after the spring frost-free date.

▸ **Best site**
Raised beds or hills where soil will warm up faster. In hardiness Zones 3 and 4, erect low tunnel greenhouses of clear plastic sheeting stretched over hoops bent from PVC pipe. If day temperatures rise to near 70° F, raise the edges of the plastic and hold them in place with clamp-type clothespins. Air can then circulate to prevent overheating.

▸ **How much to plant**
Two bushes can provide enough eggplant fruit for two people, but double that number if you like to grill and entertain.

▸ **Continuing care**
If plants begin to sprawl, buy contractor's stakes in 30-inch lengths and loosely tie the plants to them using twine. Repeat two or three times as plants develop.

▸ **Harvesting**
The tough, woody stems of eggplant fruit need to be cut with hand shears or, in a pinch, a serrated bread knife from the kitchen.

▸ **Choices**
In hardiness Zones 3 through 5, early maturity is quite important. Elsewhere, resistance to tobacco mosaic virus should be a top priority. Tender skin and slow ripening of seeds should also be considered. If you start from seeds, you have many choices in fruit color and shape. My personal favorite is 'Italian Pink Bicolor'.

▸ **Insect, pest, and plant diseases**
I have been unable to control flea beetles except by "nuking" them with chemical insecticides. For this, I make no apology to dedicated organic gardeners but will add that I apply insecticidal dust only when it is necessary and only to control this particular pest. I hope that someday, some bright researcher will come up with a short-lived botanical insecticide that will control these pesky critters.

ENDIVE AND ESCAROLE

These "kissin' cousins" add a pleasantly bitter bite to mesclun or mixed spring greens. For maximum enjoyment, begin harvesting when heads are only half-grown.

ESSENTIAL STATS

▶ **Life span**
Both are technically biennials, grown as cool-weather annuals that mature in 85–95 days from setting out transplants.

▶ **When to plant**
Very early spring planting in hardiness Zones 3 through 6 is recommended, with a second planting in midsummer. Elsewhere, cool fall or early winter weather is recommended.

▶ **Best site**
All-day full sun in cool-summer climates. Afternoon shade on late summer planting in the South and low elevations of the West.

▶ **How much to plant**
For enjoyment over a long season, begin harvesting when heads are only half-grown. Plan on 6 to 8 feet of row for two people.

▶ **Continuing care**
To blanch, gather and tie up outer leaves to shelter the heart. Heads of escarole drain better than endive and are less likely to rot from trapped water.

▶ **Harvesting**
Entire heads are usually cut off at ground level and a few of the outer leaves discarded.

▶ **Insect, pest, and plant diseases**
Endive and escarole are relatively problem-free.

KALE

Kale, like collard greens, is grown mostly for cooking. Catalogs featuring heirloom varieties offer some amazing choices of foliage, color, and leaf configurations.

ESSENTIAL STATS

▶ **Life span**
Biennial, grown as a cool-weather annual. Matures in 55 days from direct seeding in early spring.

▶ **Grow from**
Seeds germinate in only four to seven days. Direct seed thinly and transplant excess seedlings.

▶ **When to plant**
Early spring and again in mid- to late summer, depending on the length of your season.

▶ **Best site**
Kale's broad leaves can collect enough sun for it to thrive even if shaded for a few hours daily.

▶ **How much to plant**
Kale can be kept in production for several weeks if you harvest only the lower leaves, leaving a topknot of foliage to carry on photosynthesis. Plant 10 to 12 feet of row for two people.

▶ **Continuing care**
Top-heavy plants tend to topple. Push a bamboo stake down through the topknot, and press it securely into the soil. Bind the stem loosely to the stake with a plant tie.

▶ **Harvesting**
Snip off leaves, petioles and all, flush with the main stem. Wash thoroughly, and cut the petioles into ¼-inch segments.

▶ **Insect, pest, and plant diseases**
See cabbage.

KOHLRABI

Europeans and Canadians are especially fond of this cool-weather vegetable. The fleshy stem of kohlrabi is good peeled, diced, and cooked alone or with its leaves.

ESSENTIAL STATS

▶ **Life span**
Biennial, grown as a cool-weather annual. Allow 50–60 days to maturity from planting in the cold soil of early spring.

▶ **Grow from**
Direct seeding. Seeds sprout quickly.

▶ **When to plant**
Early spring and again in late summer through fall, depending on the length of your growing season.

▶ **Best site**
In full sun, away from areas shaded by the long shadows of early spring. Amend heavy soil with generous amounts of organic soil conditioner.

▶ **How much to plant**
You can plant a second crop of kohlrabi late in the season. Fifteen feet of row is good for feeding two people.

▶ **Continuing care**
Little care is needed other than twice-weekly irrigation during dry weather.

▶ **Harvesting**
Take the entire plant by cutting it off at ground level.

▶ **Insect, pest, and plant diseases**
The only serious insect pest is the green larvae of cabbageworms.

LEEK

Leeks can be grown in home gardens that are amended using plenty of organic soil conditioners. Their long growing season can tie up a planting bed from spring to fall.

ESSENTIAL STATS

▶ **Life span**
Grown as a full-season annual. Best suited to production in hardiness Zones 3 through 6. Matures in 110–125 days from setting out pencil-size seedlings in early spring.

▶ **Grow from**
Seedlings started indoors 10 weeks prior to the spring frost-free date. Transplant to the garden as soon as soil can be worked in the spring.

▶ **When to plant**
See above. In hardiness Zones 7 through 10, delay planting until the dog days of summer are past. Set them in deep furrows in garden soil amended with organic soil amendments.

▶ **Best site**
Away from flooding during spring or fall rains.

▶ **How much to plant**
A double row, 12 feet in length, is plenty for two.

▶ **Continuing care**
After two months, pile soil and organic soil conditioners around the seedlings, up to the level where the leaves turn green. Repeat once or twice.

▶ **Harvesting**
Push a spading fork to full depth beside a leek plant and pry back slowly to uproot the heavy stems.

▶ **Insect, pest, and plant diseases**
Problems rarely appear in home gardens. Some varieties claim more tolerance to frost than others.

LETTUCE

I prefer to plant seeds of leaf lettuce and butterhead types in half-and-half color mixtures. This lets me enjoy leaf lettuce while the butterhead plants are wrapping into small, tight, tender heads. Butterhead lettuce makes smaller, better-flavored salad greens than the head lettuce you buy year-round in grocery stores. In most areas, cos or romaine lettuce grows best when direct seeded in late summer.

ESSENTIAL STATS

▸ **Life span**
Biennial, grown as an annual. All types of lettuce demand cool weather and will bolt (shoot up flowering stalks) when days grow long and warm. Leaf types need 40–55 days to reach maturity but can be eaten well before full size, as "baby lettuce." The butterhead types that replaced 'Bibb' need 60–65 days to mature. Cos or romaine reaches full size in about 75 days.

▸ **Grow from**
Direct seeding. Unfortunately, lettuce isn't suited to freezing or cooking, so be conservative in your planting.

▸ **When to plant**
As soon as soil can be worked in the spring and

again in late summer for harvest during fall and winter. You can shave a month off the time required from planting to harvest by starting seeds indoors under lights and transplanting seedlings to the garden three weeks prior to the spring frost-free date, but rely on direct seeding for your main crop.

▸ **Best site**
Full sun all day for spring plantings, afternoon shade for seeds sown in the late summer. Leaf lettuce makes one of the best crops for planting in containers and for interplanting between larger vegetables.

▸ **How much to plant**
Plan on 5 feet of row for two people, or a 15-gallon pot planted with onion sets and over-seeded with lettuce or mesclun seeds.

▸ **Continuing care**
Pull out and compost the plants as soon as lettuce begins to bolt or turn bitter because of hot weather. In northern climates, it may be possible to produce short crops of leaf lettuce under shade from cheesecloth during the summer. It would be worth trying. There is no good salad substitute for lettuce during summer months.

▸ **Harvesting**
Even after two thinnings, enough lettuce seedlings should remain for using the surplus as baby lettuce. If you have an abundance of plants, cut off every other plant at ground level. But if your crop is sparse, trim or snap off basal leaves to add 10 days to the harvest season.

▸ **Insect, pest, and plant diseases**
Lettuce planted as early in the spring as the ground can be worked has few pests or diseases except cutworms and slugs. Deter both by scattering diatomaceous earth along both sides of seedling rows.

MELONS

Cultivation over many centuries has produced a wide array of melons. Two major kinds are available: watermelons and muskmelons, which include cantaloupe, honeydew, and a host of long-season gourmet melons such as Crenshaw and Casaba, which are often grouped together as "Mediterranean" melons. These are occasionally subdivided into ethnic choices such as "American," "Asian," or "European" varieties.

ESSENTIAL STATS

Life span
All are warm-season annuals. Muskmelons need from 70–85 days from direct seeding to maturity. Mediterranean kinds such as 'Crenshaw', 'Casaba', 'Santa Claus', and 'Banana' need 75–90 days to be ready for picking. These are often stored for two or three weeks after picking to ripen completely. Days to maturity for watermelons range from 75–80 days for the little "icebox" melons to 100 days or more for larger varieties.

Grow from
In hardiness Zones 3 through 5, all kinds of melons benefit from being started indoors under lights in individual pots for transplanting to the garden two weeks after the spring frost-free date. Direct seeding can succeed, especially if seeds are planted in raised hills and sheltered within plastic milk jugs with the bottoms removed. Elsewhere, melons will grow rapidly from direct seeding in warm soil.

When to plant
Rushing the season with any kind of melon can be disastrous. If late frost doesn't kill the seedlings, cold, wet soil can rot the seeds or foster fatal root rot diseases. Only in the Deep South or in low-elevation western or southwestern gardens can a second crop of melons be started in midsummer for maturity just before the fall rainy season sets in.

Best site
Select a spot that receives full sun all day. Plant in raised beds or on hills to provide a dry root run. Allow 8 to 10 feet on either side of melon plantings for the vines to ramble. Compact-vine hybrid muskmelons are available for small gardens.

How much to plant
You need at least a half-dozen plants of the variety or hybrid you choose to signal bees and wasps to come in for nectar and pollen.

Continuing care
Feeding plants after the vines have developed is difficult. Instead, work two cups of organic fertilizer into the hill before planting seeds or seedlings.

Harvesting
Most muskmelons are ready when the fruiting stem (peduncle) slips loose when you twist the melon, leaving a circular scar. Mediterranean melons and watermelons are more difficult to gauge. Often, the vines will make the decision for you and dry up, leaving no choice but to clip off the melons.

Insect, pest, and plant diseases
All melon types have their share of pests and diseases. Muskmelons are troubled by fusarium blight and powdery mildew. Some hybrids are resistant or tolerant to both. Watermelon plants often succumb to fusarium blight or have their vines damaged by anthracnose disease. Your State Extension Service can advise you on insect and disease problems.

MUSTARD GREENS

These cool-weather greens accompanied settlers from the British Isles into the southeastern colonies. Later, they were taken north when migrating workers took their food choices with them. The taste for mustard greens is still a cultural thing. In northern states, descendants of Southern families still depend on mustard and turnip greens as their primary cooked green vegetables.

ESSENTIAL STATS

How much to plant
Because you can eat the entire plant, and development is so rapid, mustard greens are one of the most efficient vegetables. They are also highly nutritious and a good source of fiber. Plan on 15 feet of row to feed two people with some left over for freezing.

Continuing care
Baby mustard greens picked during cool weather can add piquancy to salads.

Harvesting
Harvest can be extended for a few days by taking only the lower leaves. and leaving the terminal bud to produce new foliage. When mustard begins to form yellow flowers, pull out and compost the plants. At that stage the leaves become tough and too strong to eat.

Insect, pest, and plant diseases
Snails, slugs, and earwigs can decimate emerging seedlings unless they are controlled with a non-toxic (to humans) application of iron phosphate bait or diatomaceous earth. Cabbageworms can also sneak up on you and riddle leaves unless you keep a sharp lookout. Control with Bt bacteria.

Life span
In nature, mustard greens are biennial, but in gardens, they can complete their life cycle in only three months. Mustard greens are a cool-weather plant. They will flower and set a seed crop with the arrival of warm, long days, and though they can tolerate light fall frosts, a heavy freeze will wipe them out. Allow five to seven weeks to maturity from planting seeds in the garden. Baby greens can be eaten even sooner.

Grow from
Direct seeding. Seeds will sprout in four to seven days from early spring planting in cool soil.

When to plant
Early spring and again in late summer through fall, after days begin to grow shorter.

Best site
Full sun for spring plantings; afternoon shade for late summer crops. Plantings in broad, shallow containers also grow well. Plants can be squeezed into restricted open spaces between larger vegetables.

SMART *Gardener*

A superior, early maturing, slow-bolting hybrid named 'Savanna' has smooth leaves that are easier to wash free of grit than the types with curly, fringed leaves. Seed of less expensive open-pollinated varieties will produce good crops, but the stems tend to be a bit tougher and more fibrous than those of the hybrid. Press your thumbnail into the stem; if it doesn't leave a dent, strip off the blades and discard the stems. Red mustard is a favorite edible ornamental.

OKRA

Okra seeds probably came with planters and slave families from Africa to the South. It can be grown successfully in hardiness Zones 5b through 10, but the fruiting season is much shorter in northern gardens. Okra is a very productive vegetable, and one of the few that can continue producing despite very hot, humid weather.

ESSENTIAL STATS

▶ **Life span**
In temperate climates, okra is grown as a long-season, warm weather annual. Allow about 50 days from direct seeding to first pods.

▶ **Grow from**
Direct seeding in warm soil. Okra grows well on clay soil elevated on hills or ridged-up rows for good drainage during heavy summer rains. Thin plants to stand 2 feet apart. Excess seedlings can be transplanted if dug with a large root ball of soil.

▶ **When to plant**
One to two weeks after the spring frost-free date. Soak okra seeds overnight in tepid water spiked with two or three drops of dishpan detergent. Rinse well, and drain before planting.

▶ **Best site**
Daylong, full sun. Plants growing in single rows or hills can be reached from all sides for picking the pods. Place okra where it will not shade adjacent vegetables. Some varieties can grow 5 to 6 feet tall where summers are long.

▶ **How much to plant**
Two people can keep up with the production from a dozen plants, which equals 24 feet of row or four hills with three plants per hill.

▶ **Continuing care**

Okra plants are heavy feeders and will respond to a midseason side-dressing of corn fertilizer, drilled into furrows and covered with soil. Water weekly during dry weather.

▶ **Harvesting**
Harvest pods every two or three days, without fail. Pods phase from their tender "baby okra" stage very quickly. If a finger-nail pressed lightly into the stem leaves no dent, it should be discarded. Don't allow tough, over-age pods to stay on the plants and drain them of vigor. Wear cotton gloves when picking okra.

▶ **Choices**
Choose a "spineless" variety. Okra hybrids offer increased production and vigor. Hybrid 'Annie Oakley II' has dwarf plants, a distinct advantage. Heirloom varieties with red pods are available; they turn green when cooked.

▶ **Insect, pest, and plant diseases**
Okra has few pests and diseases. It can suffer from powdery mildew late in the season.

ONIONS

Worldwide, onions are one of the most important vegetables. They can be eaten at the young green stage as scallions or allowed to grow into bulbs. They can be grown from seeds, sets (immature bulbs), and seedlings. If you want large slicing or "hamburger" onions, you must start from seedlings. Young plants can tolerate all but hard freezes.

ESSENTIAL STATS

▶ **Life span**
The production of slicing onions from seedlings can take from three to four months, depending on the hybrid. "Bunching" onions are special varieties or hybrids that are sown thickly and harvested as scallions in about two months, before the stems swell into bulbs. Onion sets are small bulbs, up to ¾ inch in diameter, that are planted in early spring to produce scallions. Sets cannot produce large bulbs. 'Egyptian' or walking onions are hardy perennials that form round clusters of flowers that mature into bulbils atop the stems. The bulbils, which resemble very small bulbs, can be planted to produce green onions.

▶ **Grow from**
Most home gardeners prefer to buy seedlings to produce large slicing onions. Sets come in handy for quick production of green onions. Bunching onions with long, white stems are produced by mounding up soil around the shafts. These are the main source of scallions sold by grocery stores. Walking or topset onions are a pass-along crop, mostly given as gifts by gardening friends and family.

▶ **When to plant**
Plant seedlings or set out onion sets in early spring. Both are quite hardy. Also, where winter snow cover is dependable, or in the South and West, seeds of bunching onions can be started in late summer for overwintering for spring harvest of scallions.

▶ **Best site**
Full sun, all day, and very well-drained soil.

▶ **How much to plant**
You can't count on storing onions longer than two months, so if you want to grow big slicing onions, plant enough to share with the needy folks who depend on supplies from the food pantry. I plant three 10-foot rows close together and harvest enough to take a big boxful to our local pantry. In early spring, I plant sets in a half-barrel and inter-plant them with lettuce seeds.

▶ **Continuing care**
Onions from sets or seedlings require little care. When growing bunching onions that require mounding up soil, mulch with grass clippings to reduce erosion and slumping of soil.

▶ **Insect, pest, and plant diseases**
Root maggots and soil-borne diseases such as fusarium and pink root complicate growing onions organically. Look for disease resistance or tolerance when ordering seeds or plants, and rely on your Extension Service for advice on how to minimize insect damage. Rotating crops can help keep soil-borne diseases from building up, as can regular additions of organic soil conditioners.

PEAS *(not including Southern Peas)*

For many years, peas were grown mostly to produce green shelled peas. Flat-podded snow peas and snap peas came along much later. Now, with the popularity of Asian cuisines, more home gardeners are growing snow peas, and round- to oval-podded snap peas have become one of the most successful new vegetables ever introduced.

ESSENTIAL STATS

▷ **Life span**
Peas are a cool-season, annual vegetable. Days to maturity range from 55–70 days. The late-maturing varieties grow best in Northern states where they can mature before extremely hot weather sets in.

▷ **Grow from**
Direct seeding in early spring. It is risky to attempt a second crop of peas for fall harvest, except in cool, coastal western climates.

▷ **When to plant**
In early spring, as soon as the soil can be prepared. In clay loam soil, cover pea seeds with coarse play sand to prevent crusting and to help raise the soil temperature in the seedling furrow.

▷ **Best site**
Full sun, all day. In cool climates, standard-vine snow peas and snap peas can grow 6 feet tall and should be placed where they won't shade other vegetables. Dwarf varieties of both are available.

▷ **How much to plant**
Twenty feet of row produces plenty for two people with some left over for freezing.

▷ **Continuing care**
In windy areas, dwarf peas benefit from the support provided by "brush" saved from trimming shrubs or trees.

▷ **Harvesting**
To prevent breakage, grasp the main stem with one hand, and pick with the other. With green shell peas, pick only the pods that are swollen with seeds. You have more latitude with snow peas and snap peas.

▷ **Insect, pest, and plant diseases**
Pea wilt and mosaic virus can be carried by feeding insects. Control pea aphids with sharp sprays of water or with solutions of insecticidal soap. Severe infestations may require a botanical insecticide such as pyrethrum or Neem oil. Rotating crops can minimize soil-borne diseases such as fusarium and pythium. Control powdery mildew with Milstop.

SMART *Gardener*

With green shell peas, the most important choices are days to maturity, pod length, and disease resistance. The main-season varieties outproduce the early types but their tall vines can shade other crops. You can order dwarf varieties of both snow peas and snap peas, but they don't produce as many pods per vine as the tall varieties. Tall peas grow better on brush than on strings; their vines clamber rather than twine.

PEPPER, SWEET AND HOT

Whether you like sweet, crisp bell peppers or super-hot habaneros or chile pequins, there are peppers to satisfy all appetites. Peppers are easy to grow from seeds; easier still if you buy small plants from your garden center in the spring. Plants need little more than a regular supply of water, plenty of heat, and a long growing season.

ESSENTIAL STATS

Life span
Pepper plants can live for years in tropical climates. Over most of the US and Canada, however, peppers are grown as long-season annuals.

Grow from
Direct seeding of peppers is practical only in areas with very long, hot summers.

When to plant
Pepper plants can be killed by late frosts. Wait 10–14 days after the frost-free date before setting out plants. You can cover pepper plants with bottomless gallon-size plastic jugs to concentrate heat and protect the plants from frost.

How many plants
Four or five plants of sweet peppers can yield enough fruits for fresh use and freezing. Some gar-

deners also like to grow varieties such as anchos and poblanos for drying.

Best site
Full sun. Pepper plants won't develop well or bear bountiful crops if grown in partial shade. In areas subjected to heavy summer rains, peppers should be planted in raised beds or ridged-up rows.

Continuing care
Pepper plants like to grow in garden soil that is loosened and aerated with a generous amount of organic soil conditioner. The inclusion of pelletized limestone should prevent or minimize blossom-end rot on pepper fruits. Peppers are full-season crops. Being in the ground for several months, plants can exhaust the major nutrients in their root zones. Even controlled-release fertilizers can be used up by late summer. To give pepper plants a new lease on life, measure 12 to 18 inches out from the central stem and dig a circular furrow. Dribble ½-cup of complete organic fertilizer in the furrow and pull soil over it. Give the plants a deep watering, and continue watering every four or five days during dry spells.

Harvesting
Use hand shears to clip off peppers. Allow only a few fruits to turn red before harvest because this drains the plant of energy. When harvesting extremely pungent peppers, wear gloves and do not touch your skin or eyes.

Insect, pest, and plant diseases
Because they are distantly related to tomatoes, peppers are attacked by many of the same insects, including the ferocious-looking hornworm. Aphids can be blasted off with a sharp spray of water. Most diseases that affect peppers can be minimized by planting disease-resistant pepper hybrids and by using seeds that have been treated to kill harmful seed-borne bacteria.

POTATO

The availability of seed potato cultivars that produce crops in unusual shapes, sizes, and colors has boosted the potato's appeal both to gourmet cooks and home gardeners. The bounty that can grow from one small, budded seed piece is astounding. In garden soil modified with generous amounts of organic soil conditioner, you can routinely dig up plants with six to eight good-sized tubers plus several smaller ones.

ESSENTIAL STATS

Life span
Potatoes are grown as annuals. Seed pieces planted in early spring are usually ready for harvest by mid-summer, 70–110 days from planting.

Grow from
Seed pieces, which are sections cut from seed potatoes that are forming sprouts. Nurseries that specialize in seed potatoes grow them in fields that are kept scrupulously clean and free of diseases.

When to plant
Early spring, as soon as the soil can be worked.

Best site
Well-drained organic soil, in raised beds or containers. Potatoes grow well in cages made of waist-high fencing and partially filled with compost or spoiled hay. As the plants grow, additional compost can be sifted around them. The covered part of the stem will take root and form tubers up and down its length. Don't cover the top leaves—allow them to absorb sunlight.

How much to plant
Potatoes don't keep long in warm weather, thus are grown to be enjoyed within a month after harvest. For two people, a 15-foot row is sufficient, or four cages, 30 inches in diameter, each planted with two or three seed pieces.

Continuing care
Potato plants tend to sprawl and may need turning back. Do it carefully; the plants are brittle. Don't be concerned if your potatoes form small, light purple blossoms. If the tops of any tubers show above the ground, scatter soil on them to block sunlight that can turn them green.

Harvesting
Potatoes will keep better in the ground than on your kitchen counter, so harvest only a plant or two at a time. However, if an extended period of rain is forecast, dig all of them to prevent the tubers from rotting in the ground. When the potato vines fade to yellow-green and stop growing, it is time to dig beside one plant and feel around for tubers. If the tubers seem to be large enough, pry around with your spading fork and see what is exposed. After picking up the exposed tubers, feel around for ones that may have been left behind. Potatoes keep if gently brushed off, wrapped individually in newspaper, and stored in a cool place.

Insect, pest, and plant diseases
Unsightly "potato scab" can occur when potatoes are grown on high pH soil. You can reduce its incidence by scattering a light dressing of agricultural sulfur when you set out the seed pieces. Invasions by potato beetles are common. Gardeners with just a few potato plants can pick them off by hand. Neem oil sprays can be effective but the beetles tend to drop off and scuttle away when sprays shake the foliage.

PUMPKIN

Many gardeners are acquainted with the great variety of pumpkins, from the miniature Jack-O'-Lantern types through the behemoth 'Dill's Atlantic Giant'. Some pumpkins resemble winter squash, some winter squash resemble pumpkins. A quick way to tell them apart is to look at the stem. If, in cross section, the stem is hard and five-sided, it is a pumpkin. If it is round and either soft or corky, it is most likely a winter squash.

ESSENTIAL STATS

Life span
Pumpkins are warm-season annuals that need from 95–120 days to produce mature fruit. A recent hybrid, 'Neon', is ready for picking in 65–70 days.

Grow from
Direct seed in hills or ridged-up rows to provide a well-drained root run. Allow plenty of room for the vines to run: typically, pumpkin vines span 20 feet or more. Seeds should germinate in five to seven days.

When to plant
Wait a week or so after spring frost danger is past.

Best site
At the back of the garden where the rampant vines won't impede foot traffic. A good slope will help keep summer rainwater from standing and rotting fruit.

How much to plant
Unless you are growing pumpkins for Halloween decoration, one or two hills with three plants each will suffice. The larger the fruit, the fewer each vine will bear. Small-fruited varieties can be run up small trees or fences, but large fruited kinds must spread on the ground.

Continuing care
With bees and wasps becoming scarce, you may have to assist pumpkins in the pollination required to form fruits. Go out early in the morning and look for female blossoms, notable for their slighty swollen fruiting stems. Male blossoms will show yellow or golden pollen. Use a camel's-hair brush to transfer pollen from male to female blossoms. You may have to do this several mornings in succession to find just-opened female blossoms at prime stage for accepting pollen.

Harvesting
Pumpkins are ready when the vines begin to turn

yellowish-brown. Clip them off using hand shears, leaving enough fruiting stem to serve as a handle.

Choices
Pumpkins range in shape from the typical round or oval shapes on sale for Halloween to drum-shaped and flattened, top to bottom. Colors are mostly in the yellow-orange range, except for the types grown for their seeds.

Insect, pest, and plant diseases
Squash bugs can severely injure pumpkin vines, and powdery mildew can blight vines late in the season. Neem oil can control both if you begin spraying when you see the first squash bug. But squash bugs are notoriously tough; you may have to resort to the dreaded chemical controls to exterminate them.

RADISH

Radishes are the speed demons of the vegetable garden, ready for eating in only four to five weeks from planting. The colorful roots spice up the look and flavor of salads.

ESSENTIAL STATS

▶ **Life span**
Technically biennials, radishes are grown as cool-season annuals. Seeds can germinate in as little as four to five days.

▶ **Grow from**
Direct seeding. Radishes excel in sandy soil or in the porous soil of containers. When planting in heavy soil, make furrows and drill in the seeds; then cover them with ¼ inch of coarse play sand.

▶ **When to plant**
Early spring for harvest during cool weather. A second planting can be made in early fall for harvest before cold, wet weather stops growth. Large Daikon varieties grow best in hardiness Zone 8 through 10, where they are seeded in late summer for harvest the following spring.

▶ **Best site**
Raised beds or containers in full sun all day.

▶ **How much to plant**
Radishes mature all at once; so plant only short rows at two-week intervals to extend the harvest season.

▶ **Insect, pest, and plant diseases**
Radishes are in and out so quickly that few insects trouble them. Flea beetles can be a problem, also pillbugs that can attack the foliage near ground level. Overcrowding is the most prevalent problem.

RHUBARB

Rhubarb is the only vegetable able to tolerate a half-day of shade. The long, ridged, red stems are the edible part; eating the leaves can cause digestive upsets.

ESSENTIAL STATS

▶ **Life span**
A hardy perennial that can live for many years, rhubarb is best equipped for cold-winter climates, especially where snow insulates its crowns and where good drainage discourages rotting.

▶ **Grow from**
Vegetative divisions taken from mature crowns.

▶ **When to plant**
Late spring or early fall is the best time for planting. Fall plantings should be mulched.

▶ **Best site**
The east side of a building is best, where rhubarb can escape the burning afternoon sun. Work in lots of organic matter garnished with organic fertilizer when preparing the site for planting.

▶ **How much to plant**
Three crowns of rhubarb will give you enough stems for the occasional pie, plus some for freezing.

▶ **Continuing care**
Always leave two or three stems when harvesting to rebuild food reserves in the roots. Feed plants organic fertilizer in early summer. Dress mulch around the plants after the first frost of fall but don't fertilize late in the season. Cut off any flowering stems.

▶ **Harvesting**
Cut stems 1 to 2 inches above the crown, making sure not to slice into the crown.

SOUTHERN PEAS (a.k.a. Cowpeas)

Southern peas is the name used by most seed breeders to describe this group of heat-loving, beanlike vegetables. Cowpeas can withstand prolonged heat and humidity.

ESSENTIAL STATS

▶ **Life span**
Warm-season annual. Allow about 70 days for southern peas to mature.

▶ **Grow from**
Direct seeding in warm soil. Difficult to transplant.

▶ **When to plant**
In early summer, when all danger of frost is past.

▶ **Best site**
Full sun, all day. Southern peas can adapt to many soil types, and can succeed as far north as Zone 6.

▶ **How much to plant**
You will need about 20 feet of row to feed two people. The green seeds freeze easily, so plant accordingly.

▶ **Continuing care**
If you choose to grow a variety with rampant vines, consider interplanting them with sweet corn. The pea vines will plug along slowly until the cornstalks dry, then they will grow rapidly, using the stalks for support. The corn will benefit from the nitrogen produced by beneficial bacteria at the pea roots.

▶ **Harvesting**
Pick and shell pods in the morning.

▶ **Insect, pest, and plant diseases**
Southern peas can succumb to root diseases and nematodes in the soil. Rotate crops, and maintain good levels of organic matter in the soil.

SOYBEAN (a.k.a. Edamame)

Many years ago, David Burpee introduced edible soybeans in his seed catalog. They never sold well until Japanese cuisine caught on in North America.

ESSENTIAL STATS

▶ **Life span**
A warm-season annual, grown much like garden beans. Allow 65–75 days to maturity.

▶ **Grow from**
Direct seeding in rows 30 inches apart. Seeds sprout in five to seven days.

▶ **When to plant**
In warm soil one week after the spring frost-free date.

▶ **Best site**
Full sun, all day. Edamame thrives in clay-loam soil.

▶ **How much to plant**
Plant two rows back to back so the plants can help support each other. Fifteen feet of double row should yield enough pods to feed two people.

▶ **Continuing care**
Edible soybeans need little care and can get by with an inch of rain or irrigation per week. Don't let plants wilt during hot, dry, windy weather.

▶ **Harvesting**
I prefer to plant an early variety such as 'Early Hakucho', which matures all its pods at much the same time and can be picked in one pass. The easiest way to pull the pods off the vines is to pull up the plants one at a time and strip off the pods.

▶ **Insect, pest, and plant diseases**
I have had few problems with growing edamame. Armyworms and velvetbean caterpillars can trouble the plants, but they haven't found mine yet.

SPINACH

Here is a vegetable that rivals broccoli in popularity. While spinach is most often planted as a spring crop, it shines as a fall crop. Plants may overwinter and produce a crop the following spring. Use a plastic sheet to warm up the soil in colder regions. The young leaves of spinach can be added to salads; mature leaves can be cooked.

ESSENTIAL STATS

▶ **Life span**
Cool weather annual with outstanding winter survival, except where winters are very cold and snow cover is scant.

▶ **Grow from**
Direct seeding with seeds that have been soaked overnight in tepid water spiked with one or two drops of dishpan detergent. Rinse, drain, and plant immediately. Cover the primed seeds with ¼ inch of coarse play sand.

▶ **When to plant**
Early spring in hardiness Zones 3 through 7, and again in late summer. In the Deep South and low elevations of the West, late summer plantings can yield harvests throughout the winter and into early spring. Allow 40 to 60 days from planting to harvest readiness; spring plantings mature faster.

▶ **Best site**
Spinach prefers well-drained soil. This is especially important if crops are expected to live over winter.

SMART *Gardener*

The most important trait to look for in spinach is slow bolting. The growing seasons for spinach are marked by fluctuating temperatures that can force some plants in spinach populations to shoot up flower stalks earlier than others. Bred-in resistance to bolting, such as in 'Bloomsdale Longstanding', can make a significant difference in production. 'New Zealand Spinach' (Tetragona expansa) for summer greens is available from Jung Seeds but has never caught on with the gardening public.

Spring-planted spinach prefers full sun all day. Spinach planted in the heat of late summer through early fall can benefit from the shade cast by trees that lose their leaves in the fall, when temperatures drop.

▶ **How much to plant**
Ten feet of row can feed two people.

▶ **Continuing care**
Spinach seeds usually have a good percentage of germination. Two or three thinnings may be necessary to open up plantings enough for plants to grow to full size.

▶ **Harvesting**
Remove only the basal leaves by pinching off the leaf petioles near the main stem. This will extend the harvest season to as much as four weeks.

▶ **Insect, pest, and plant diseases**
Slugs, snails, and earwigs can devour seedlings as they emerge. Control them with a light dusting of a bait laced with iron phosphate. Plants can show symptoms of mildew in humid weather. Control it with a benign fungicide, such as Milstop.

SQUASH

The young fruits of summer squash are delectable, whether fried, grilled, or steamed with onions and bacon crumbles. Among these, 'Crookneck', 'Straightneck', and 'Zucchini' are traditional favorites. And where would we be without the hard-shelled winter squash for baking and for steaming to make squash soup?

ESSENTIAL STATS

Life span
Both tender-skinned summer squash and hard-shelled squash are warm-season annuals. Expect the first harvest from summer squash in 45–55 days from planting. Winter squash takes up to 100 days from direct seeding.

Grow from
Grow summer squash from direct seeding a week or two after the spring frost-free date. You have more latitude in planting dates for winter squash, especially where summers are long. Squash seeds are often planted 3 or 4 to a hill.

Best site
Full sun all day for both types of squash. Summer squash plants are robust and can spread to a diameter of 4 or 5 feet. Winter squash vines can ramble as much as 20 feet.

How much to plant
Two or three plants of summer squash can feed two people, with plenty left over for freezing. Harvest the fruits when they are young and tender. All the fruits of winter squash will be ready at about the same time. Bring them inside if a hard frost is predicted. Wrap them in newspaper and store them in a warm, dry place for as long as five months.

Continuing care
With honeybees on the wane, summer squash may need hand pollination. See "Pumpkin," page 117 for directions. Winter squash sets blossoms over a longer period, and beetles and flies supplement pollination. Winter squash can benefit from a mid-season drench of water-soluble organic fertilizer.

Harvesting
Cut off summer squash using a long, sharp, flexible knife. If any fruits fail to pass the thumbnail test, cut them into pieces and put them in the compost heap. With winter squash, delay harvest until the vines turn brown and dry, or until just before the first hard fall frost. The fruits need to stay on the vines as long as possible to develop full flavor.

Insect, pest, and plant diseases
Unfortunately, two of the most serious vegetable pests plague plants of squash. Squash vine borers, the larvae of a small moth, bore out the center of stems and cause them to wilt. Damage is most serious on summer squash. Squash bugs, shield-shaped green or brown evil-smelling insects, inject a wilt disease as they feed, and entire plants can die. Some of the chemical insecticides can kill them. Hopefully, someone will come up with a reliable, organically acceptable control. The only control for squash vine borers is to slit the stems where you see frass (excrement) extruded, and pull out the larvae one by one with a wire hook. Covering the wounded stem with soil sometimes helps.

SWEET POTATO

If sweet potatoes could talk, they would ask not to be called "yams." A poorly informed but imaginative promotional company, eager to boost sales of Louisiana-grown sweet potatoes, gave them that name. True yams are the large, rough-skinned, white-fleshed roots of tropical species of vines.

ESSENTIAL STATS

Life span
In North America, sweet potatoes are grown as a warm-weather, full season annual, and need 85–100 days from transplanting to harvest.

Grow from
"Slips," which are rooted plants that grow from sweet potato roots sunken in warm soil. If you want just a few, buy potted slips. For mass plantings, buy rooted slips by the bunch, usually 50–100 count.

When to plant
Wait until two weeks after the spring frost-free date in your hardiness zone. If your slips arrive earlier, pot them up temporarily to harden them off in a protected, sunny corner.

Best site
Full sun all day. Sweet potatoes produce best on moderately fertile soil. If you pamper them too much, they can produce too-big roots. In heavy soil, ridge-up rows to give the plants a well-drained root run.

How much to plant
Sweet potato vines, except for the compact cultivars, can spread as widely as winter squash. If you are short on garden space, you can train the vines up a low, temporary fence to reduce their spread. Six vines can feed two people, but if you can grow more, take the surplus to a local food pantry.

Continuing care
Gently lift each vine by the tip and pull up gently to weed the area. Flip the vine toward the center (crown) of the plant; take out the weeds using a scuffle hoe; and then lay the runners back where you found them.

Harvesting
To maximize production and size, wait until light frosts have browned the foliage. Probe gently with a spading fork, 18 inches from the crown of the plant, and pry up. If you meet no resistance, move in closer and try again, being very careful not to spear or abrade the roots. Shake or gently brush soil off the roots. Find a warm spot, such as a shed where sun heats the air, and lay the roots out to cure, not touching one another. In about two weeks, the roots should have lost sufficient moisture to keep for a month or so. When they begin to sprout, bake, peel, and freeze them for making sweet potato dishes and pies during the winter.

Insect, pest, and plant diseases
Sweet potato weevils are a continuing problem in the Deep South, and are so serious that USDA plant quarantines forbid shipping plants from affected areas. Pathogenic nematodes are also a problem. Several fungal diseases can attack stored roots. These problems are less severe in more northerly gardens. Go to the Internet for advice from your State Extension Service for controlling insects and diseases of sweet potatoes.

SWISS CHARD *(a.k.a. Chard)*

The reigning king of summer greens, Swiss chard has gained considerable popularity, thanks to the development of several flashy leaf and stem colors. Basically a leaf beet, it has been selected for tenderness, flavor, and crisp, succulent leaf blades. Swiss chard seeds are actually corky fruit containing several seeds. Use the leaves in the same way you use spinach.

ESSENTIAL STATS

Life span
Technically a biennial, chard is grown as a full-season annual. It can stand a few degrees of frost, even in the seedling stage.

Grow from
Direct seeding or, if you need only a few plants, from six-packs of seedlings. Sow seeds thinly, as plants need to be spaced 6–9 inches apart to flourish. Soak seeds overnight in tepid water spiked with two drops of dishpan detergent. Rinse, drain, and dry on newspaper just enough to let you scatter the seeds thinly. Priming the seeds will cut three or four days off the time required for germination. Allow 50–60 days to first harvest.

When to plant
A week prior to the spring frost-free date is plenty early, and you won't risk losing the seedlings to a late, hard freeze. Scatter slug and snail bait as soon as seedlings emerge.

Best site
Full sun all day, although chard can tolerate either morning or afternoon shade, thanks to the sun-trapping nature of its broad leaves.

How much to plant
Plant only short rows unless you have a definite taste for chard. Try substituting it for spinach in cooked dishes.

Continuing care
Thin direct-seeded chard two or three times, and add the thinnings to salads as baby greens. Chard transpires a lot of soil moisture through its broad leaves and can benefit from mulching.

Harvesting
Use a sharp knife to cut the leaf blades about 2 inches above soil level. Give the blades the thumbnail test; trim off and compost the tough part.

Insect, pest, and plant diseases
Beet pests cross over to chard. The worst of these is beet leaf miner. Cut off infested foliage, and bury it in your compost heap to keep this pest from spreading. Controls are ineffective because the pest is hidden between layers of cells. Tarnished plant bugs can also build up populations. Caterpillars will occasionally roll foliage over themselves, but one pinch per caterpillar will cure that problem.

TOMATO

Tomatoes are the most popular garden edible, and justifiably so. The bland taste of tomatoes shipped over great distances is enough to convince people with enough sunlit space to plant a few tomato vines. While I advocate and plant hybrid tomatoes for their higher production and improved disease resistance, I understand why gardeners plant several kinds of heirloom tomatoes for their different flavors and colors.

ESSENTIAL STATS

▶ **Life span**

Tomatoes are grown as warm-season annuals. They can be injured by light frosts. Days to maturity from setting out seedlings range from 65 days for early varieties or hybrids to 80–90 days for the later-maturing, large-fruited kinds.

▶ **Grow from**

Seedling plants. While it is possible to grow tomatoes from direct seeding, the cost of seeds, in particular seeds of hybrids, makes it impractical. Start seeds indoors under lights eight weeks prior to the spring frost-free date and transplant seedlings to individual pots for "growing on" prior to setting them in the garden.

▶ **When to plant**

Set out seedlings a week after the frost-free date. They will adjust better to garden conditions if hardened-off in a protected corner where they can get sunlight and are protected from winds and frost. This extra step will help plants perform better.

Best site

Some kinds of tomatoes can grow quite tall and will need support from posts or cages. These cast shade, but if placed on the east side of the garden, the shade won't fall on nearby plants. Tomatoes respond to organic soil conditioner worked into the soil before setting out plants. To reduce blossom-end rot, incorporate one cup per plant of pelletized dolomitic limestone into the soil at planting time; two cups where the soil is very acid. This is also a good time to work a cup of organic fertilizer or ½ cup of controlled-release fertilizer into the root zone of each transplant.

How much to plant

Healthy plants of hybrid tomatoes can produce 30–60 pounds of tomatoes per plant, some ripe, some green, when you glean the plants at the end of the season. Half that amount would be closer to the national average. It follows that three or four plants would produce far more fruit than a family

of two could eat fresh. But the surplus can be canned. If it is your first try at canning, go to the Internet for instructions, and follow them exactly to ensure food safety.

Continuing care

Tomato vines should not be allowed to sprawl on the ground, even when you have mulched around them. The flimsy cylindrical frames sold as tomato cages are not up to the task. Six- to 8-foot-high cylinders constructed of steel reinforcing mesh are best. Make them with a diameter of 30 inches, and keep them from blowing over by wiring each cage to a steel post driven a foot deep into the ground. The large mesh also permits reaching inside to pick fruits close to the central stem.

Harvesting

Some tomato varieties or hybrids have an easy-picking gene, and the fruiting stem separates easily from the cluster or "hand" of fruit. Others have to be twisted off, and with considerable effort. It's best to snip them off using hand shears. Small-fruited tomatoes have no such problem; in fact, cherry tomatoes tend to drop off the cluster when ripe. Tomatoes don't store well in the fridge. Keep them in a bowl on the counter so you can enjoy them with every meal. When a surplus threatens, either take them to your local food pantry, or break out the deep kettle, jars, and lids needed for water-bath or pressure-cooker canning.

Insect, pest, and plant diseases

As befits the most popular crop, tomatoes have their share of problems. Foremost is "blossom-end rot," caused by fluctuating levels of soil moisture and a shortage of available calcium and magnesium in the soil. Planting hybrids with bred-in resistance or tolerance reduces foliage and systemic diseases. Of the diseases, tobacco mosaic virus is the most serious, followed by early and late leaf blight, and root system diseases caused by fusarium, pythium, and rhizoctonia organisms. Various species of nematodes can build up to harmful levels, especially in the South. Collectively, these are reasons to consider growing tomatoes in large containers such as half-barrels, raised off the ground and filled with commercial potting soil. If nematode damage persists in your garden, consider buying predatory nematodes. Problems with tomato hornworms are less serious. All you have to do is muster the courage to pick up these alarming-looking caterpillars and dispatch them.

TURNIP AND TURNIP GREENS

Many civilizations have depended on turnips stored in root cellars or pickled in brine or vinegar as a winter food source. In this country, generations of southern gardeners have relied on turnip greens to nourish them through hard winters. Now, the challenge is to educate a wider audience to appreciate turnip greens, cooked in broth or perhaps with just a bit of ham or bacon, and not boiled to death.

ESSENTIAL STATS

▷ **Life span**
Turnips are biennial, grown as a cool-weather annual. In my experience, turnips are second only to collards for winter-hardiness. Roots can be ready to eat in 40–50 days, depending on the date seeds are planted. Greens can be ready even faster.

▷ **Grow from**
Direct seeding. Turnip seedlings don't take well to transplanting. Plant seeds in shallow furrows, and cover them with coarse play sand to get germination in three to four days.

▷ **When to plant**
Early spring as soon as the soil can be worked, and again in late summer for fall and winter harvest.

Early-summer plantings can result in foliage that is too strong to eat and stringy, fibrous roots.

▷ **Best site**
Full sun all day, in well-drained soil.

▷ **How much to plant**
Twelve feet of row can easily feed two people and provide a small surplus for freezing. Thin turnips rigorously. Cook the thinnings.

▷ **Continuing care**
Turnip plants are survivors and will tolerate neglect. But keep an eye on your crop, and don't let it lack water, or both greens and roots can drop in quality. Where winters are quite cold, after light fall frosts have driven field mice into hiding, spread a straw mulch over turnips to prevent the roots from freezing. No mulch is needed further south. You can store turnip roots in the ground for perhaps two months.

▷ **Harvesting**
To extend the harvest of turnip greens, nip off petioles of outer leaves where they join the root, saving the center growth to maintain photosynthesis. When growing turnips for roots, pull out every other plant to leave room for the remainder to develop. Harvest all of them before they begin to develop a "bite" and excess fiber. Try mixing turnip and mustard greens. The mild-tasting mustard greens can take the edge off the taste of turnip greens.

▷ **Insect, pest, and plant diseases**
Root maggots and root aphids can disfigure turnip roots. Aphids can distort foliage buds and leaves. Rotating crops and planting turnips in soil generously amended with organic matter can reduce problems with soil insects. Crops that mature in the fall usually have fewer problems with pests than spring-planted turnips.

Selected Fruits

7

Selecting Fruits

There are several species of fruit that are compatible with vegetables and that can be grown within vegetable gardens. In general, these are small fruits that grow on vines or bushes and require less spraying for insects and diseases than fruit that grows on trees, such as apples, pears, and peaches.

With the rising cost of fresh fruit, however, I expect more gardeners to consider adding fruit trees to their landscapes. Space permitting, I recommend that you try growing fruit-bearing trees, adding a few kinds at a time as you learn how to care for them. Most fruit trees can be pruned and trained to remain short for easy access. Compared with the few varieties in the supermarket, the range of available tree-fruit cultivars is immense. The trees are relatively costly, and there's many details to

consider before you make a selection: winter hardiness; chilling hours, which helps plants break dormancy and grow at the same time; which kinds make good companions to ensure pollination; inbred disease resistance; harvest time; and keeping quality. I can't stress too strongly the need to familiarize yourself with information on the particular fruit you wish to grow. Start with your State Extension Service, and see the Resource Guide beginning on page 184 for more recommendations.

Finally, a note about oranges, lemons, limes, and the many other species and hybrids of citrus fruit. While these are undoubtedly of great importance, they can only be grown successfully in hardiness Zones 9 and south and in Hawaii, and their requirements are very different from those of deciduous tree fruits. For these reasons, we have chosen not to cover citrus and other frost-tender tropicals in this book.

Gathering raspberries for a delicious breakfast.

Fresh, fragrant peaches, perfectly ripe.

SELECTING, PLANTING, *and* MAINTAINING
Fruit Trees

1. **Consult your mail-order source** or local Extension Service to make sure that the cultivars you like are suited to your climate. The farther north you live, the more important it becomes to select late-flowering cultivars that escape most late frosts.

2. **Order two or more cultivars** that flower at the same time to ensure the pollination required for fruit set.

3. **Decide whether you want** fully-dwarf, semi-dwarf, or standard-size trees.

4. **Opt for a cultivar recommended** by your Extension Service as resistant to diseases found in your area.

5. **Make sure that the site you choose** is in full sun, is open to breezes, is well-drained, and is not in a frost pocket.

A cherry tree in bloom.

6. **Prepare the soil for planting.** You may be advised that the best soil to fill in around trees is the soil you dug out of the planting hole. This applies only to deep, loamy, well-drained soils. With most garden soils, your trees will grow better if you first remove or kill existing grass and weeds in a circle 6 feet across. Next, mix in a 3-inch layer of premoistened peat moss or other organic soil conditioner and organic fertilizer according to the manufacturer's directions. Then dig a planting hole about 2 feet across and deep enough to accommodate the tree's roots after pruning off dead or damaged roots. Position the roots on a cone of soil at the bottom of the hole, and spread them over this soil. This will keep the crown from settling below ground level later. Lay a board or stick across the planting hole to see whether the crown is elevated enough. Finally, use the prepared soil to fill in around the roots and up to the level of the soil line.

7. **Brace the new tree.** Leaves will pop out on newly planted fruit trees before their roots have spread widely enough to support the tree against strong winds. Buy two 6-foot pieces of steel rebar, and drive them 1 foot deep into the soil, 1 foot away from the trunk and across from each other. Stretch several lengths of twine between the rebar supports 2 or 3 feet above the soil level, encircling the trunk on each pass. This will restrain the tree from breaking or wiggling loose yet will allow it to flex and develop strength.

8. **Varmints, insects, and diseases.** Deer can be deterred from rubbing their antlers on tree trunks by bracing the tree. (See step 7.) Later, you may have to erect deer fencing. Guard against mice and rabbits by loosely wrapping the bottom 6 inches of the trunk with hardware cloth. Different species of fruit-tree insects are troublesome in different areas. Some can be lured into traps, but others require sprays that will not kill the bees, flies, and wasps that are vital for pollination. Sprays of light horticultural oil applied during the dormant season will minimize peach-leaf curl and insect pests. Garden centers sell dual-purpose concentrates that can be diluted and sprayed on fruit trees.

APPLE

Early settlers brought apple seeds with them to the American colonies, not for eating the fruit so much as for distilling the pressed juice into cider—the harder, the better. In fact, Johnny Appleseed planted many varieties favored for cider making during his travels through the frontier. Apple trees remain a favorite for new gardeners.

ESSENTIAL STATS

▶ **Life span**
Apple trees can live as long as two centuries. Many large, old trees have been replaced with newer dwarf or semi-dwarf grafted cultivars.

▶ **Grow from**
Trees are sold either in containers or bare-root. Bare-root trees are shipped in the spring or late fall in the South and West.

▶ **Adaptability**
Consult your State Extension Service and local botanical garden for cultivars adapted to your area.

▶ **How to plant**
Either plant a bare-root tree as soon as it arrives, or place it in a 5-gallon container of potting soil. Water the containerized plant every day or two until late summer. Then plant, mulch, and water every week thereafter until winter. Bare-root trees will need to be watered twice weekly while new leaves are breaking out, and weekly thereafter. In hardiness Zone 5 and north, set out new bare-root trees in the spring so they form extensive root systems before very cold weather arrives.

▶ **Years to first crop**
Apple trees take three to five years to bear a significant crop of fruit.

▶ **Continuing care**
Prune trees annually in the dormant season to shape into an open form that allows access for spraying and harvesting.

▶ **Recommended cultivars**
'Cortland', adapted to Zones 3–8, is a favorite all-purpose apple cultivar. Another old-timer, 'Wolf River', has good disease resistance.

'Liberty' and 'Pristine' are immune to apple scab and resistant to cedar-apple rust, fireblight, and powdery mildew. 'Sweet Sixteen' is resistant to cold, scab, and fireblight.

▶ **Harvesting**
Dropped fruit (called "falls") are usually bruised and should be used only for making juice or cider. Invest in a canvas bag with a shoulder strap to free your hands for picking as you climb a ladder. For large trees, buy a telescoping fruit picker. Unblemished fruit should be wrapped in newspapers and stored in a cool, shaded area or in the refrigerator.

▶ **Insect, pest, and plant diseases**
While it's possible to grow apples organically, it takes much knowledge and skill. A reasonable alternative is an Integrated Pest Management Program of traps, horticultural oil sprays, and insecticides.

BLACKBERRY (Thornless, Hedge Type)

Blackberry bushes naturally bear small fruit on rangy, thorny plants. The bushes spread by roots that emerge about 1 foot away from the mother plant. Home gardeners will appreciate the new sweet, large-fruited, thornless cultivars, which can be grown as freestanding specimen plants or hedges.

ESSENTIAL STATS **1-3** ➕ -

▷ **Life span**
Bushes grown in food gardens are usually renewed every few years, using rooted sprouts from the perimeter of established plants. The old plants may be dug out, but you might require an herbicide.

▷ **Grow from**
Bare-root plants are shipped in early spring. Container plants are sometimes available from large nurseries, but they will probably not be the newer hedge cultivars.

▷ **Adaptability**
Blackberries are among the many species that require warm days and cool nights in order to set fruit. They can be grown in hardiness Zones 6 through 9. Some cultivars may tolerate greater extremes of summer or winter temperatures.

▷ **How to plant**
Invasive grasses can ruin berry patches. Make sure that all perennial grasses are either destroyed using herbicide or removed, roots and all. Incorporate plenty of organic soil conditioner, lime where necessary, and organic or controlled-release fertilizer prior to planting. Mulch around the canes using 2–3 inches of hardwood bark to suppress weed and grass seedlings. If signs of nitrogen drawdown show in yellowing of plants, give them a shot of liquid fertilizer. Repeat if necessary.

▷ **Years to first crop**
Allow the erect bushes to grow to about 4 feet in height, and shear off the growing tips. Lateral branches will form and will bear fruit in early summer of the following year.

▷ **Continuing care**
During the winter, remove the canes that bore fruit the previous year. New shoots will have formed among the old ones. Shear off the tips of the new shoots, and they will bear fruit the next season.

▷ **Recommended cultivars**
Currently, 'Apache' and 'Arapahoe' are two thornless patented cultivars. Because other kinds of blackberries have become nuisance crops in California and Hawaii, these plants cannot be shipped there.

▷ **Harvesting**
For eating fresh or freezing blackberries, wait a few days after fruits have turned purple-black and are juicy and sweet. For making jams or jellies, a mixture of ripe and nearly ripe fruit is recommended. Thornless varieties make harvesting much easier.

▷ **Insect, pest, and plant diseases**
One of the best preventative practices against mites and fungi is a spray of light horticultural oil when the vines are dormant. A good time to apply it is soon after winter pruning. Check your State Extension Service Web site for advice.

BLUEBERRY

Blueberries are one of the easiest of the bush fruits to grow, although they demand acid soil. Some of the modern cultivars combine impressively large berries with excellent flavor. I've seen cultivars taller than me, but they needed 10 years to grow to that size.

ESSENTIAL STATS

Life span
Blueberry bushes can live and produce bountiful crops for many years.

Grow from
Three-year-old bare-root plants are shipped by mail-order sources. Larger plants in containers are occasionally available from well-stocked nurseries.

Adaptability
High-bush and rabbit-eye types of blueberries can be grown from Lower Michigan to Florida. Low-bush cultivars survive better in areas where snow cover hangs on for most of the winter, protecting the low, fruiting buds. Rabbit-eye types are more often seen in the Southeast. Blueberries thrive in the Pacific Northwest.

How to plant
Blueberries need acid soil, in the 5.5–6.0 pH range. When you have your soil tested by your State Extension Service, let them know that you intend to plant blueberries. They will tell you whether you need to apply agricultural sulfur and, if so, how much per bush. Use a mulch of chipped wood or bark.

Years to first crop
Four years after setting out 3-gallon-size plants, I am just now getting significant crops.

Continuing care
Dress granular organic fertilizer over the root zone of each plant. Reapply 2 inches of mulch annually. Dig or pull weeds or grass while they are still small. In soils that test higher than pH 6.0, scatter some agricultural sulfur around your blueberry bushes every two or three years, and use acid-forming fertilizers.

Recommended cultivars
'Northland', a hybrid between low-bush and high-bush varieties, is good for hardiness Zones 3 through 6. For very large berries, 'Patriot', like 'Northland', is super-hardy. You will have better

pollination if you plant two or more cultivars that bloom simultaneously.

Harvesting
Don't forget to spread bird netting over frames, and check it often for holes and tears. For maximum flavor, wait for two or three days after berries turn blue. When picking, massage the clusters gently, and the dead-ripe fruits will come loose in your hand. Repeat every four or five days.

Insect, pest, and plant diseases
Perhaps the most frustrating insect pests to home gardeners are those that deposit eggs in young blueberry fruit. The larvae are referred to as blueberry maggots. Tiny insects known as thrips can deform plants by gathering and feeding in the buds of leaves and fruits. Should you notice stunting of plants, it could be due to a disease carried by a species of leafhopper. Your State Extension Service can advise you on a preventative spray program.

CHERRY

Few new gardeners know that, in addition to the large, dark, very sweet cherries sold in supermarkets, there are sour-cherry cultivars available that are excellent for making pies. Large red, black, or yellow sweet cherries are slightly less tolerant of heat and extreme cold than pie cherries. Most sweet cherries produce better if planted near a different cultivar known to be a good pollinator, such as a pie cherry.

 **ESSENTIAL STATS**

▶ **Life span**
Cherry trees are not particularly long-lived but will often produce well for decades.

▶ **Grow from**
Grafted "whips"—slender 3- to 5-foot-high cultivars—are shipped bare-root in spring at a date determined to be safe for planting in your zip code. Some garden centers order bare-root fruit trees for early delivery and plant them in containers for sale after the whips have sent out new feeder roots. Generally, container-grown trees can be planted more safely later in spring or summer than bare-root specimens.

▶ **Adaptability**
Most pie cherries grow well in hardiness Zones 5 through 7. Catalogs offer a few cultivars that will survive winters in Zone 4 and others that will tolerate Zone 8 summers. Large sweet types are well adapted to Zones 5 through 7 and marginally in Zone 8.

▶ **How to plant**
See general planting instructions for fruit trees.

▶ **Years to first crop**
I harvested a small crop of cherries the third year after planting my self-pollinating cherry tree.

▶ **Continuing care**
Pruning cherry trees has evolved into a science, and you should consult the Internet or your local library for instructions. The canopy needs to be sparse enough for you to see through it and free of branches that grow inward or cross each other. Above all, start early, and watch results carefully. Certain cherry cultivars top out at a height of 10 to 12 feet. Bird netting is necessary, so the smaller the tree, the easier the job.

▶ **Harvesting**
Tasting cherries is a better way to judge their readiness than trying to judge by their color. Pie or tart cherries will keep for only a few days, so plan to allot time for preserving and freezing. Sweet cherries will keep for a maximum of a week or so in the refrigerator, so be prepared to share the surplus with friends or your local food pantry.

▶ **Insect, pest, and plant diseases**
Leaf spots, aphids, the larvae of various flies, Japanese beetles, and scale insects are some of the most prevalent problems. Keeping your trees clean organically is difficult. Most gardeners value their cherry crops so much that they prefer to apply all-purpose fruit sprays on schedules developed by their Extension Service.

CURRANT

Now that interest in foods containing antioxidants and vitamin C is increasing, more nurseries are offering good selections of currants. Although many species are native to North America, most cultivars grown for their fruit originated in Europe. The clusters of fruit resemble small, translucent grapes.

ESSENTIAL STATS 1-3

Life span
Plants can live for decades if pruned each fall.

Grow from
Plants ordered from catalogs are shipped bare-root in the spring.

Adaptability
Like the gooseberry, its close cousin within the genus *Ribes*, currant is hardy well up into Canada. It grows best in humid climates with relatively cool summers. Currants will grow well in full sun or light shade part of the day.

How to plant
Currant grows best in slightly acid soil in raised beds for good drainage. Adding and digging in premoistened sphagnum moss acidifies soil while improving drainage. When planting black currant, cut back each shoot to 3 buds to increase branching, and prune out old shoots every year. Black currant sets fruit better if you plant more than one cultivar. Spring-planted, bare-root plants have to be nursed through their first summer with frequent watering. Consider potting-up bare-root plants in 3-gallon plastic pots filled with potting soil, set near a faucet so they can be watered regularly. After the hot, dry months have passed, you can plant the now-well-rooted plant in its permanent location.

Years to first crop
Currant plants will set good crops of fruit two seasons after planting.

Continuing care
Red and white currant plants set fruit on old wood. Prune only when they fail to set good crops of fruit. Apply mulch or compost 3 inches deep at planting time, and refresh with more mulch every fall. If rodent damage beneath heavy snowfall is a problem, cover lower stems with hardware cloth.

Recommended cultivars
You can choose between black, red, white, or blush pink cultivars. Even though the attractive color of red cultivars such as 'Red Lake' and 'Jhonkeer' has long been favored, the exceptional levels of antioxidants and Vitamin C in black cultivars such as 'Ben Sarek' are winning over gardeners. White currants such as 'Blanka' are prized for winemaking.

Insect, pest, and plant diseases
Fourteen states will not allow currants or gooseberry plants to be sold because of white pine blister rust, which infects plants from the genus *Ribes*. The currant borer and the gooseberry fruit worm are two of the worst insect pests. Aphids can be controlled with a spray of insecticidal soap or neem oil, but the more serious pests need protective sprays applied on a schedule available from your State Extension Service.

FIG

Hardly a farm in the South or the valleys of California is without a fig tree. The amount of fruit I picked and ate as a boy exceeded that which reached the house.

▷ **Life span**
Fig trees can live for several decades.

▷ **Grow from**
Fig trees are usually grown in containers and sold at a height of 3–4 feet.

▷ **Adaptability**
Figs are reliably hardy north through Zone 7. Fancy large-fruited cultivars grow best in the warm valleys of California.

▷ **How to plant**
Fall is the best time for planting in the West and Deep South; spring in the middle to upper South. Water frequently until new growth appears. Once established, trees need deep watering every two weeks during dry spells.

▷ **Years to first crop**
From two to five years, depending upon the size when first planted.

▷ **Continuing care**
Mulch is recommended, but should not be piled up around the trunk. Scatter organic fertilizer prior to adding a new layer of mulch.

▷ **Recommended cultivars**
'Celeste' was the cultivar we planted at Victory Garden South in Georgia. 'Brown Turkey' is still quite popular in the Southeast.

GOOSEBERRY

Gooseberries were traditionally grown for use in pies and preserves because they were too tart for eating fresh. New cultivars are sweet enough to eat out of hand.

ESSENTIAL STATS 1-3

▷ **Life span**
Gooseberry bushes can live for 20 years.

▷ **Grow from**
Gooseberry plants are usually shipped as bare-root 2-year-old plants.

▷ **Adaptability**
Gooseberry prefers cool summers. It will grow in hardiness Zones 3 through 7, but plants will produce more in the northern half of this area. Plant in spring in Zones 3 and 4.

▷ **How to plant**
Gooseberries grow best in raised beds of clay loam soil that have been modified with premoistened peat moss.

▷ **Years to first crop**
Expect your first light crop the second year after transplanting to the garden.

▷ **Continuing care**
Plants can tolerate morning or afternoon shade. Some cultivars are thorny and should not be planted where they might injure people or pets.

▷ **Recommended cultivars**
Choose between red cultivars such as 'Hinnomaki Red' and 'Poorman'. White cultivars include 'Invicta' and the golden 'Hinnomaki Yellow'.

▷ **Insect, pest, and plant diseases**
Gooseberry and currant are closely related, and troubled by the same pests and diseases.

GRAPE *(Wine and Table)*

Two North American species, *Vitis labrusca* and *Vitis rotundifolia,* are used for juices and jellies. The European *Vitis vinifera* produces great wine and table grapes.

ESSENTIAL STATS 1-3

▶ **Life span**
With careful pruning, grape vines can live for decades.

▶ **Grow from**
Mail-order catalogs provide the widest choice of cultivars; their plants are usually shipped bare-root in the spring.

▶ **Adaptability**
For most cultivars, hardiness Zones 5–9. Some concord cultivars can withstand winters in Zone 4, and many muscadine types thrive in Zones 7–9.

▶ **How to plant**
Bare-root vines should be set out in well-drained soil in the spring, after frost danger is past, and watered frequently to ensure a good set of feeder roots. Container plants should be set out as described for fruit trees in this chapter.

▶ **Years to first crop**
A light crop can be expected in the third year.

▶ **Continuing care**
Unless you plan to train a vine up an arbor, you can set a post in place and plant the rooted cutting beside it.

▶ **Insect, pest, and plant diseases**
Consult your State Extension Service for organic or Integrated Pest Management information.

KIWIFRUIT, HARDY

This vining type of kiwifruit can be grown in cold climates. It has smooth skin and fruits the size of large grapes. The hardy, green-leaved species *A. arguta* is preferred for fruit production.

ESSENTIAL STATS

▶ **Life span**
Hardy kiwifruit plants can live for 50 years.

▶ **Grow from**
Bare-root plants are shipped to arrive after the danger of spring frost is past.

▶ **Adaptability**
Hardy kiwifruit is best adapted to areas with cold winters and relatively cool summers, but it'll grow and produce in hardiness Zones 4 through 7. The vines need good drainage to survive cold winters.

▶ **How to Plant**
Prepare soil by digging-in a generous amount of organic soil conditioner. Install a tall post at the site, and plant the kiwifruit close to it. Tie the vine to the post using strong twine. As the plant grows, set two or three more posts about 6 feet apart, and connect them with strong wire. Within two years, the vines should cover this framework.

▶ **Years to first crop**
Hardy kiwis should begin producing within three to four years following planting.

▶ **Continuing care**
Wrap the lower 4 feet of the central trunk with tree tape down to ground level to protect it from damage due to thawing on sunny winter days.

▶ **Insect, pest, and plant diseases**
For excellent information, see "Growing Kiwifruit," published by Oregon State University.

PEACH

Wild peaches are as common in the Southeast as crabapples are in the Northeast. Peaches grown at home and picked at their peak taste far better than those that are shipped unripe from far away. Peaches are self-pollinating, so unless you experience several days of rain during bloom time, you should get good fruit set. Most modern varieties offered by mail-order nurseries are resistant to peach-leaf curl.

ESSENTIAL STATS **1-3**

Life span
Despite control programs, insects usually attack peach trees and destroy them after 10 to 20 years. Plan on planting a new tree every five years or so.

Grow from
Bare-root trees, 3 to 5 feet in height, are shipped to arrive in early spring; late fall in the Deep South and warm West.

Adaptability
Peaches grow well in hardiness Zones 5 through 8, except where local conditions favor late frosts. The genetic dwarf peach cultivars grow and produce

well in containers, but in Zone 6 and north, you will need to shelter them during the winter.

How to plant
Peaches bloom so early that they grow best on a south slope with sun-warmed soil and excellent air circulation. Except for their vulnerability to frost at blossom time, they are relatively simple to grow.

Years to first crop
Peaches can bear a handful of fruit the second year after planting.

Continuing care
Thinning fruit clusters is recommended. Otherwise, you risk deformed fruit and fungal damage.

Recommended cultivars
'Redhaven', a large-fruited, freestone cultivar is a favorite among peach growers in Missouri. 'Reliance' is more cold-hardy. An old cultivar with soft fruit and white flesh, 'Belle of Georgia', is one of the best-tasting peaches I have ever eaten.

Harvesting
Peaches don't ripen all at once. The best time for picking is two or three days prior to fruit beginning to soften and drop.

Insect, pest, and plant diseases
Even cultivars resistant to peach-leaf curl can become susceptible with age and will need two dormant-season sprays with lime-sulfur or horticultural oil. Brown rot is always a threat where summer humidity is high. Continue preventative sprays until just before harvest. Gathering dried-up fruit from under the tree gains additional control after harvest is complete. Double-bag the "mummies" and leave the sealed bag in the sun to compost. The heat should kill the spores of the brown rot fungus. Don't put this in your compost heap; bury it instead. All-purpose fruit tree sprays can help control Oriental fruit moths and borers.

PEAR

Pear cultivars come in two major types—European and Asian. The European types are more winter-hardy and include many familiar pears developed to eat fresh. Skin colors when ripe range from green and yellow to red and russet. Asian types are often apple-shaped and have russet skin similar to 'Bosc' pears.

ESSENTIAL STATS 1-3

Life span
It is common for pear trees to live at least 50 years.

Grow from
Unless you have a spacious landscape, select dwarf cultivars that mature at a height of 12 to 15 feet. Standard pear trees grow quite large and need to be pruned, beginning the first winter after planting.

Adaptability
Refer to your State Extension Service or local botanical garden to determine which pear cultivars are suitable for your garden. Also, almost all cultivars need to be planted with another cultivar that blooms at approximately the same time.

How to plant
See the general directions for planting fruit trees. Pollinator trees are most effective if planted within 20 to 30 feet of their companion trees.

Years to first crop
Technically, pear trees can begin bearing fruit the third or fourth year after planting. Standard-size trees need a year or two longer than dwarf types to set significant crops of fruit.

Continuing care
All pear cultivars need pruning every winter to keep their canopies open and to remove water sprouts and dead or diseased branches. You might have to tie a brick or two to branches to bend them down. Mulch with spoiled hay or straw, but do not pile the mulch up around the trunk. If soil is poor, dress organic fertilizer over the old mulch before adding a new layer. Fertilize in midsummer to avoid tenderizing the tree to winter cold.

Recommended cultivars
Fruit sizes range from the smallest, 'Seckel,' through the 1½-pound fruits of the heirloom cultivar, 'Atlantic Queen'.

Harvesting
Most European-type pears ripen on the tree. 'Comice' is an exception. It should be picked just before fall frost and brought indoors for ripening. Asian pears are usually picked and ripened indoors; some will keep for months in cool storage.

Insect, pest, and plant diseases
Choose cultivars resistant to fireblight and scab diseases, especially if gardening organically. Resistance to a disease caused by a species of Pseudomonas is important in the Northwest.

POMEGRANATE

There has been an explosion of pomegranate products recently, mostly due to its healthful properties. Pomegranate is rich in antioxidants and flavinoids, which may protect against heart disease. They are self-pollinating; single plants will set good crops. Their vulnerability to cold limits them to warmer climates.

ESSENTIAL STATS

Life span
If planted in well-drained soil and watered every 10 to 14 days, pomegranate bushes will live for several decades.

Grow from
Containerized pomegranate bushes are sold year-round in garden centers in zones where they are hardy. Mail-order nurseries ship bare-root plants after danger of spring frost is past.

Adaptability
Pomegranates grow best in the warm interior valleys of California and at low elevations in the Southwest in heavy, moisture-retentive soils, where the bushes can be irrigated. They will also grow well in hardiness Zones 8 through 10.

How to plant
Plant in full sun, or in areas with afternoon shade in desert areas. Set plants at least 10 feet apart to provide room for the spreading bushes.

Years to first crop
Allow three to four years from setting plants in the garden to the first significant crop. Well-established bushes can yield 8 to 12 pounds of fruit.

Continuing care
The pomegranate's brilliant red fruit makes a strong visual statement. Radical pruning may remove the year-old wood on which fruit is borne. Gardeners should remove dead growth at ground level to keep the bushes from becoming "thickety" and should prune away inward-growing branches to keep the canopy open.

Recommended cultivars
The cultivar 'Eversweet' is esteemed not only for earliness but also for its high percentage of pulp. In long-season areas, pomegranate aficionados prefer 'Pink Satin'.

Harvesting
In hot, dry areas, the fruit may split if left on the bush or tree too long. Elsewhere, the fruits are nipped off using pruning shears and taken indoors when frost is predicted. Store fruit in a cool, dry place. Even though hard-shelled, the fruit should be handled carefully. Halve the fruits; scoop out the seedy pulp; and run it through a blender to make juice.

Insect, pest, and plant diseases
Pomegranates have few problems. In humid areas, powdery mildew on tender terminal growth can be controlled with neem oil or Milstop sprays.

THERE ARE SEVERAL SPECIES OF SMALL FRUITS that are compatible with food gardens but that most North American gardeners have never seen, much less grown. Some are natives of Europe or Asia; others species are native to North America. Some grow as shrubs, others as small trees. The ones that intrigue me the most look attractive, have tasty fruits, and require little pruning and minimal pest controls. All need full sunshine and well-drained soils.

ARONIA OR CHOKEBERRY (*Aronia*)

I first grew aronia as an ornamental shrub, primarily for its brilliant autumn foliage and bark color. I wasn't aware that its fruit was edible until I sampled some. Tart, but good! Long ago, European plant breeders began selecting and hybridizing species of this native North American shrub, and lately, US breeders have begun introducing cultivars bred for heavier crops of larger fruit. They aren't concerned about the tartness because it is due to very high concentrations of vitamin C. Aronia is a triple-threat ornamental, with white flowers in the spring, followed by clusters of purple-black fruit the size of blueberries, and orange-red fall foliage. The plants are self-fertile, grow to 4 to 6 feet in height, and don't require pruning. Resistant to both cold and summer heat, aronia will grow well in Zones 3 through 9. Aronia has few serious pests but needs netting against birds.

SEA BUCKTHORN (*Hippophae rhamnoides*)

Although little known in North America, sea buckthorn is the most widely grown, northern-hardy fruiting plant in the world. Adapted to Zones 3–9, this small, thorny tree requires "two to tango." The female tree will bear prodigious crops of small, golden or orange fruit in heavy clusters. Too tart for eating out of hand, the fruits are used for juice, sauces, and jellies, alone or blended with other kinds of fruit. The Internet may provide feedback from home gardeners who have tried this species.

PAWPAW (*Asimina triloba*)

This is a large shrub native to North America, not the tropical papaya, which is also called "pawpaw" by some. Wild pawpaw populations can be found in forests from Florida to Michigan. Thanks to the recent interest in sustainable agriculture, this carefree native shrub has been extensively improved for winter hardiness and larger fruit. Depending on the cultivar, pawpaw fruit may range from 6 to 12 ounces. When fully ripe, the fruits have a custard-like consistency and a flavor reminiscent of bananas. They are high in vitamins A and C. They prefer organic, slightly acid soils that aren't allowed to go dry during the summer. Other than hungry animals, paw paws have few problems. Trees are not reliably self-fertile, so you will need two.

SERVICEBERRY or SHADBUSH (*Amelanchier*)

When I planted an unnamed cultivar of native serviceberry in a bed of small shrubs and perennials, I intended it for a spring bloom and brilliant fall color. That it bore edible fruit was secondary. However, when it had grown to about 8 feet high, a heavy crop of fruit surprised me. To my delight, I harvested more than 5 pounds of berries the size of large peas and froze most of them for winter use. The berries were sweet when eaten fresh; the interior stones were tender and crunchy. I use them on cold cereal during the winter. My tree suffers a bit from cedar-apple rust and loses a few leaves, but its health has not been greatly affected.

RASPBERRY

Most raspberry cultivars have thorny canes and are inescapably labor-intensive. Still, I've never seen raspberries on sale for less than two or three times the price of strawberries at their peak season. So if you like raspberries, grow your own and save money. In general, raspberries grow and produce best in cool-summer climates.

ESSENTIAL STATS 1-3 ❄ -

▶ **Life span**
Healthy clumps can live for 10 to 20 years. Buy only virus-free plants.

▶ **Grow from**
Some catalogs sell "plugs" of raspberries. These are small, well-rooted plants. Container plants are available in Zones 4 through 6.

▶ **Adaptability**
Raspberries grow best in relatively cool summers. Four major types are available: the native American black raspberry; red raspberry; purple cultivars; and yellow raspberry. Red raspberry is the most winter hardy. Black, purple, and yellow cultivars are not reliably hardy north of Zone 4.

▶ **How to plant**
To avoid exposure to virus diseases, kill any wild raspberry or blackberry plants growing nearby. Also, do not plant raspberries in old vegetable gardens that could be infested with verticillium, a soil-borne disease. Choose a site that receives full sun all day. Prepare planting hills or raised beds with a

generous amount of organic matter for good drainage and aeration. Set the plants so that their crowns are 1 or 2 inches lower than the surrounding soil, and water them weekly until they form feeder roots.

▶ **Years to first crop**
With care in soil preparation, raspberries can set a few berries the second season after planting.

▶ **Continuing care**
Each plant produces two kinds of canes: new growth, and fruiting (old growth). Cultivars are either "summer/June bearing" or "everbearing." During the fall dormant season, cut off the canes of summer-bearing cultivars that bore fruit the previous season. The following spring, thin out the weak canes to leave three or four vigorous canes per plant. In addition to taking out spent fruiting canes, prune new growth on these cultivars back to a length of 24 to 36 inches. To avoid having to construct trellises for everbearing raspberries, do a cut-back pruning every winter. In the fall of the following year, prune off all spent fruiting canes at ground level. Everbearers can bear fruit on one- and two-year-old wood.

▶ **Recommended cultivars**
Check the Internet for lists of cultivars that are recommended by your State Extension Service.

▶ **Harvesting**
Depending on summer heat, raspberries can be ready from early July through August.

▶ **Insect, pest, and plant diseases**
Virus diseases can be carried in the tissue of plants that have been infected by aphids. Start with virus-free plants from a reputable nursery, and maintain a spray program that doesn't allow aphids to get a toehold. If rust disease shows on any plant, dig it out and dispose of it, but not in the compost pile.

STRAWBERRY

You have to taste the difference between homegrown and store-bought strawberries to understand why so many home gardeners opt for strawberries over all other small fruit. Almost all homegrown and locally produced strawberries are smaller but far more flavorful than the shipped-in kinds.

ESSENTIAL STATS 1-3

▷ **Life span**
Plants can be counted on for two years of production.

▷ **Grow from**
Many strawberry plants are sold in 4-inch peat pots by garden centers.

▷ **Adaptability**
Most cultivars are hardy from Zones 3 through 8, but a few are restricted to Zones 4 through 8. Strawberries need full sun all day, but in Zones 7 and 8 they can benefit from afternoon shade.

▷ **How to plant**
All strawberries benefit from being planted in raised beds on soil modified using plenty of organic soil conditioner. If you grow only a few plants in a hill or in a container, you can maximize production by meeting their nutrient needs using a controlled-release fertilizer.

▷ **Years to first crop**
When set out in the spring after the danger of killing frost is past, they can produce a pretty good crop late the first year.

▷ **Continuing care**
Snip off all runners as they begin to form on spring-planted, everbearing cultivars to encourage the development of the clusters of blooms called "crowns." Also snip off all blossom clusters that form prior to midsummer. Rooted satellite plants taken from the ends of runners and planted in a new raised bed "catch" quickly and reliably and produce a good crop the first full growing season. The University of Illinois Web site provides good information on growing strawberries.

▷ **Recommended cultivars**
Ask your State Extension Service for a list of June-bearing or everbearing cultivars that have performed well in your area. At present I am growing the everbearing cultivar 'Tristar'. Among the cultivars that intrigue me is 'Cabot', for its large, flavorful, red berries.

▷ **Harvesting**
Choose deep-red, fully ripe fruit, and discard any that are overly mature. I kneel on a padded bench and pick using one hand while parting the foliage with the other. When I have picked a row, I go back and look again. Usually I find several ripe berries overlooked on the first pass.

▷ **Insect, pest, and plant diseases**
Birds take a few of my berries, as does a hungry three-toed box turtle that returns every year to my strawberry patch. I do move my strawberry beds around my garden and plant only virus-free starts. Verticillium wilt can infect strawberries growing on garden land that has been in production for years, but compost and organic fertilizers, along with no-till gardening, should help to avoid that problem.

Selected Herbs

8

Learning About Herbs

At one time, my wife and I had 3 acres of herbs in production and two sizable greenhouses on a farm in South Carolina. We even tried winter production in Mexico. Ultimately, though, trying to deny the old adage for success—location, location, location—finally did us in. We just couldn't compete with the many local herb growers whose businesses were closer to their restaurant customers.

One important legacy I did retain from this experience was an interest in using herbs in my own home cooking. I talked frequently with major chefs who shared their secrets for incorporating herbs in recipes and as garnishes. I also learned techniques for growing, harvesting, and drying herbs.

Another thing I came to observe was that many gardeners aren't sure of the difference between vegetables and herbs. Basically, I consider vegetables to be an ingredient in an entree or side dish. Culinary herbs function as the seasoning for vegetables, meats, fish, poultry, and, occasionally, desserts.

Savory herbs, such as rosemary, basil, oregano, and thyme have strong flavors that hold up through cooking. They are commonly used in soups and stews and with meats such as wild game, duck, goose, and fatty roasts. In centuries past, the assertive aromas of these herbs were used to mask the "off" flavors of meat that was past its prime. More delicate herbs, such as arugula and fennel, are often used as side dishes or in salads.

What Size Herb Garden?

How many herb plants you grow and how large a space you devote to them depends on how much you use them for cooking and garnishes. Many gardeners prefer to scatter herb plants among their ornamentals or to grow them in containers. If you are squeezed for space to grow food crops, you should start out small with herbs until you find out which flavors you prefer and how many plants of each you need for fresh use, freez-

ing, and drying. All herbs grow well in containers, but don't try mixing highly aggressive mint or lemon balm with the nonaggressive herbs. Guess which species will crowd out the others? Perhaps most important is that almost all culinary herbs prefer full sun all day long, and that all reach their full potential when grown in well-drained soil (mint included).

Scores of books filled with herb lore line the shelves of libraries, and the romantic background of many herbs can be enchanting. Discipline yourself to try perhaps one new herb yearly, and if it doesn't prove useful, out with it!

A decorative bee skep serves as a charming focal point of this small herb garden, opposite. Planted as part of a food garden or ornamental landscape, herbs add a range of shapes, hues, and delightful fragrances, below.

ARUGULA

A distant relative of mustard greens, arugula is an herb that is often used as a salad green. When grown during cooler weather, arugula has a flavor that has been described as a cross between peanuts and soybeans. In growing arugula, the object is to maximize the production of tender leaves. As the plant ages, the larger leaves impart a stronger bite.

ESSENTIAL STATS

▶ **Grow from**
Arugula should be direct seeded in early spring and again in late summer. Grow in fertile soil amended with plenty of organic matter.

▶ **Continuing care**
Water regularly to keep the soil constantly moist, especially during hot, dry spells. Lack of moisture intensifies arugula's peppery bite.

▶ **Harvesting**
Start cutting as soon as the plants reach 3 inches. Use scissors to trim the plant 1 inch above soil level, leaving a base that will regrow and produce fresh leaves. For maximum freshness, harvest just before eating, or store in the refrigerator in a plastic bag.

Culinary TIP

In early summer, arugula plants form flowers and small, greenish-red seedpods, both of which are edible. Mix with lettuce, endive, or Napa cabbage for a tasty treat in tossed salads.

BASIL, SWEET

I was surprised to learn that many more varieties of basil are used in Asian cooking than in Mexican or Italian cuisine. The purple varieties of basil make attractive purple-pink vinegars and flavored oils. Lemon basil is also popular in gourmet cooking but tends to quickly shoot up flower and seed stalks.

ESSENTIAL STATS

▶ **Grow from**
Sow indoors 4–6 weeks before final spring frost. For direct seeding, wait until soil temperature is at least 60°F and all danger of frost is past. I often buy small plants that allow me to harvest fresh basil nearly a month before I could enjoy the crop grown through direct seeding.

▶ **How to plant**
Plant in a warm, sheltered spot with well-drained soil. Keep soil moist, and protect plants from slugs.

▶ **Continuing care**
All basils are frost-tender and require frequent removal of flower buds to encourage vegetative shoots. Basil is one of the best late-season food sources for bees, but the first light frost will kill the plants. Plants can grow as high as 5 feet tall in warm climates.

▶ **How much to plant**
I have found that three plants of basil can give me all the fresh basil I can use in one season and plenty for drying.

▶ **Recommended cultivars**
Some chefs regard 'Genoa Sweet' or 'Genovese' as the best green basil. It grows quickly and easily from seeds sown in the garden well after frost danger is past. 'Magic Michael' is the most ornamental, with purple leaves and flowers.

Culinary TIP

When using dried basil in salads or fruit dishes, be sure to crumble it to a dust-like consistency and to remove stems. Wait until just prior to use before pulverizing basil; the crumbling process releases volatile oils, which can be lost in storage.

CHIVES

Common chives are more useful than garlic chives, a different species of the genus *Allium*. Cut chives flush to the ground to eliminate yellowed tips on new growth.

▶ **Grow from**
This hardy ornamental perennial can be grown from seeds or started plants. Allow chives a year to become established before harvesting. Plants will live for years, spreading slowly.

Culinary TIP

If you grow gourmet varieties of potatoes such as Yukon Gold or Fingerling, dress them with chopped chives for a mild, scallion-like flavor. The pink blooms of chives are also edible.

▶ **How to plant**
Set out potted plants, or direct-seed in the spring. Cover seeds lightly with soil to improve germination. Thin seedlings to 6–8 inches apart. Sow every three weeks for a continuous supply.

▶ **Continuing care**
Clumps of chives can live for years, but the center growth tends to die out. Every few years you should dig out all your chives; pull apart the congested clumps; and replant small clumps of three or four bulbs. Cut chives close to the ground after they flower. That way, you don't have to sort out woody flowering stems from the new growth.

CILANTRO

Cilantro is essential to Hispanic and Asian cuisines. The dried seeds of cilantro are the spice known as coriander. Try freezing cilantro for use in a pot of hearty winter chili.

▶ **Grow from**
Cilantro can be grown from seeds the same way you would grow dill. Cilantro does not transplant well, so direct-seed into the plant's final position.

▶ **How to plant**
Cilantro will grow in sun or partial shade in normal soil enriched with some organic matter.

▶ **Continuing care**
Keep a supply growing during hot summer months by sowing a few seeds every two or three weeks and using the young plants, roots and all. Once hot weather arrives, the plant quickly forms flower stalks and completes its life cycle. Cilantro plants can tolerate light frosts.

▶ **Recommended cultivars**
'Delfino' has finely divided leaves that make an attractive garnish. 'Leisure', which is slow to bolt, is bred primarily for leaf production.

Culinary TIP

Cilantro resembles flat-leaf parsley enough to fool many people when they are hurrying through the supermarket. When in doubt, just crush a leaf and sniff, and you will have no further confusion. I use a lot of cilantro in salads and bean dishes. The plump, green seeds can be chopped and used also.

DILL

The fern-like leaves and umbrella-shaped flowers of fresh dill add a touch of grace and distinctive fragrance to a food garden. Dill adds a nice touch to pickled vegetables.

ESSENTIAL STATS

▶ **Grow from**
Dill is a short-lived, frost-tender, cool-weather annual. It does not transplant well; direct-seeding is best. Dill grows well in containers and as a quick-turnover herb for interplanting.

▶ **How to plant**
Plants do best in full sun all day. Direct-seed soon after spring frost danger is past; cover lightly with soil to improve germination. Dill will tolerate many soil types but grows best in clay loam soil. Keep the bed moist, and thin seedlings to 6–8 inches apart. Ten plants are more than enough for a family of two to four.

▶ **Continuing care**
Dill flowers quickly, and the plants dry up during the long days of summer. Dill can tolerate only a few degrees of frost. I direct-seed dill about every three weeks in summer for a continuous supply. Dill plants may host the larvae of black swallowtail butterflies. Allow an extra plant or two for their rations.

▶ **Recommended cultivars**
'Fernleaf', which quickly grows to only 18 inches high, is useful in small beds or flower borders. 'Dukat' (also known as 'Tetra'), is a cultivar that was developed to be slow to bolt.

FENNEL

The herb known as sweet, wild, or Sicilian fennel is a tall, elegant plant that possesses the same anise flavor as the vegetable variety of fennel but lacks its bulb-like base.

ESSENTIAL STATS

▶ **Grow from**
Sweet fennel is a short-lived, semi-hardy perennial. It will grow well from direct-seeding from early spring through late summer, or in fall in southern gardens, if temperatures stay above 60°–65° F. Fennel prefers moist, deep soil but copes well in free-draining soils, too.

▶ **Continuing care**
Cut leaves when they are large enough to use. Seeds can be gathered once they have dried. In mild climates where seeds can survive the winter, remove the flowers before they shed their seeds to prevent from spreading. Fennel is a perennial in Zone 6 and south.

▶ **Recommended cultivars**
Sweet fennel is prized for adding an anise flavor to dishes. Bronze fennel makes a tall, beautiful orna-mental with edible foliage. Florence fennel is a type that forms a "bulb" (actually clasping stems) that can be cooked by steaming with butter.

Culinary TIP

Fennel bears a superficial resemblance to dill, but its foliage and seeds are anise-scented. The seeds are popular as breath fresheners in some Middle-Eastern and South Asian cultures.

GARLIC

You may never have considered growing garlic because of its wide availability, but this relative of the onion is a hardy perennial that is quite easy to grow.

ESSENTIAL STATS

▶ Grow from
Garlic never produces seeds, so the best way to propagate it is to save cloves from the previous season. Plant the cloves 3 inches deep in well-drained soil from late summer through fall. Shoots will emerge from the cloves in about a month and live over winter. Additional leaves will form the following spring as bulbs develop under the soil.

▶ Continuing care
When the foliage has yellowed and begun to dry, dig the bulbs up out of the soil and let them dry in the sun for two to three weeks. Store the bulbs in a dry place before fall rains prompt them to re-grow. Some of the bulbs will be smooth, round, and without segments. Most will divide into cloves.

"Rounds" can be eaten as is but are usually replanted soon after harvest, to produce cloves the following harvest.

▶ Recommended cultivars
'Silverskin' is most often found in grocery stores. 'German Red' and 'Spanish Rioja' grow well in colder climates. Varieties such as 'California Late' and 'Early Italian Red' thrive in warm temperatures.

AROMATIC *Lavender*

YOU SHOULDN'T FORGET THE SCENTING HERBS when planning your herb garden. Of these, **lavender is the most important.** It is hardy north through Zone 5 and even farther north where the ground is covered with snow for much of the winter. The trick in succeeding with lavender is to **begin with started plants of a proven cultivar, such as 'Provence' or 'Lady',** having prepared either a raised bed or raised mounds to give the plants excellent drainage. **Lavender needs a soil with near neutral or slightly basic pH level.** Wait until three weeks after the average spring frost-free date to set out plants (fall planting is recommended in the South and warm West.) After planting, spread an inch of white sand to cover an 18-inch circle around each plant. **The sand will reflect light up into the plants and increase photosynthesis.** To groom plants for the coming season, wait until late spring before nipping off branches ½ inch beyond the outermost new buds. Pruning too early, followed by warm weather and then a late frost, can be fatal to lavender plants. I recommend starting with at least three plants to provide plenty for drying. Reserve a plant or two in the event that soggy soil causes some plants to die.

LEMON BALM

Lemon balm, a sturdy, hardy perennial, is a member of the mint family. The fresh leaves make a delightful tea with a hint of citrus flavor.

ESSENTIAL STATS

Grow from
Lemon balm is customarily started from container plants after danger of spring frost is past. Plants are available in dark green or golden foliage colors and will grow to a height of about 2 feet in full sun.

Adaptability
Hardy in Zone 4 south through 7 (Zone 8 when given afternoon shade.) In warm areas, this herb is a perennial and will self-seed.

How to plant
Lemon balm will grow in most soils. In hot areas, provide some shade from midday sun, particularly for the yellow and variegated types.

Continuing care
Grow in containers, and clip off flower heads before they drop seeds. Many gardeners rue the day they turned this aggressive herb loose in their gardens. Once established, lemon balm plants will spread in your garden from roots and seeds. Cut down old foliage, and lift and divide the plant in the fall.

Culinary TIP
Lemon balm's sharp piquancy recommends it for flavoring fruit pies and teas.

MARJORAM

Sweet marjoram (*Origanum majorana*) is closely related to oregano. French chefs often combine it with parsley, tarragon, and chives for a seasoning known as *fines herbes.*

ESSENTIAL STATS

Grow from
Marjoram can be easily propagated from cuttings. You can also direct seed in mid-spring, which will result in good-size plants before fall frost. Plants will grow to a height of 10 to 14 inches and will produce distinctive, bead-like flower buds and sprays of white blooms. Several plants are needed to produce enough of the top growth for drying. Set plants in herb gardens or containers after frost danger is past.

Adaptability
Marjoram is hardy up to Zone 6, where it can be treated as a perennial; in colder areas, treat it as an annual.

Continuing care
Marjoram plants need little care except watering during dry spells. They are occasionally bothered by leafhoppers, which can be controlled with neem oil spray. Wait 10 to 14 days before harvesting sprayed foliage.

Culinary TIP
Marjoram's subtle aroma and flavor are more evident in the fresh product than in the dried foliage. Add marjoram toward the end of cooking to get the most from its delicate taste.

MINT

While refreshing as a flavoring, mint is also an attractive but aggressive landscape plant. It is a perennial, so you can expect plants to last for years with minimal care.

ESSENTIAL STATS

Grow from
Grow all mints from started plants of named cultivars, of which there are legion. Plant in a large container in a rich potting mix—simply inserting cuttings just below the soil surface will be sufficient for growth.

Continuing care
Keep plants well-watered, and feed with a balanced liquid fertilizer. If grown in a container, they do best in partial shade or full sun. Because they are such vigorous growers, container plants run out of steam after a few years. Repot every one to two years, replanting some of the newer rhizomes that have formed in fresh potting mix. Water containers frequently. All mints are winter hardy. Peppermint has a sharper flavor and is preferred for making mint juleps. Many of the mints have seductive names but prove of little use in the kitchen.

Culinary TIP

Perennial spearmint is the most popular mint for flavoring drinks, sauces, and cooked dishes. Peppermint has more bite and is favored for making mint juleps, tea, and herbal infusions.

OREGANO

There are more than 40 species in the genus *Origanum*, many of which are used for seasoning. Others are ornamentals or grown for drying and use in winter bouquets.

ESSENTIAL STATS

Grow from
Purchase potted plants or take divisions from established clumps. Crush and sniff a leaf before you invest in a plant. Oregano makes such a dense mat of growth that occasional digging and dividing will help to produce more vegetative growth.

Culinary TIP

Oregano is one of the few herbs that is stronger dried than fresh and it is the easiest of the herbs to dry. (See How to Dry Herbs, page 159.) 'Italian' oregano is the favorite among chefs. 'Greek' oregano's strong flavor complements Middle Eastern dishes.

When to plant
Throughout the growing season in the South and warm West, so long as you water plants frequently until they are well rooted. In Zone 5 and north, plant in late spring to avoid winterkill.

Continuing care
Clip off blooming stems to force more vegetative growth. Shear off the outer 6 inches of runners for drying. The young tips have the best flavor.

Adaptability
Oregano rarely lives through winter north of hardiness Zone 7.

PARSLEY

Traditionally used as a garnish, parsley's tasty, nutritious leaves are also delicious when chopped and blended into soups, salads, sauces, and vegetable dishes.

ESSENTIAL STATS

▶ Grow from
Usually grown from plants, as it is slow to start from seeds. A biennial, parsley may survive the winter but will usually shoot up flower stalks and die after completing its life cycle the following spring. Parsley seeds need approximately three weeks to germinate.

▶ When to plant
Set out hardened-off plants in early spring; they should be able to stand up to late frosts. Plants can be set out later, but they will need frequent watering until established. Parsley does better in cool, partial shade and in fertile, moist soil.

▶ Continuing care
If there were an ideal plant for containers, it would be parsley. The plants are compact and recover quickly after their lower leaves are harvested. Parsley also looks beautiful in the food garden.

Culinary TIP

You can buy fresh parsley all year long, but a sure way to have fresh sprigs when you need them is to grow your own. Freeze pureed parsley in ice-cube trays and add to hot soups and stews.

ROSEMARY

Rosemary's needle-shaped leaves and pale blue flowers make this tender, evergreen shrub a lovely landscape plant in hardiness Zones 8 and 10.

ESSENTIAL STATS

▶ Grow from
Rosemary grows slowly from seeds, so most gardeners buy good-size started plants to maximize harvests. 'Arp', named after a town in Texas, is regarded as one of the hardiest cultivars.

▶ Adaptability
While it is possible for rosemary to overwinter in hardiness Zone 5, it rarely happens. A site with perfect drainage and shelter from drying winds is the key.

▶ Continuing care
In temperate climates, rosemary plants need little attention when grown in well-drained soil. If brought indoors and kept in a cool, well-lighted room, rosemary might hang on until spring.

▶ Recommended cultivars
I grew 'Tuscan Blue' as a landscape plant on our South Carolina farm; it reached up to 5 feet tall.

Culinary TIP

Sprigs of rosemary are easy and quick to dry, and they taste great when used to flavor meats, vegetables, oils, or vinegars. Use your fingers or a knife to break up dried rosemary leaves before adding to a recipe. Experienced chefs can tell the difference between rosemary cultivars by their fragrance.

SAGE

Culinary sage has a distinctive aroma that for many summons memories of Thanksgiving turkey. However, many sages are grown as ornamentals and have little flavor.

ESSENTIAL STATS

▶ **Grow from**
Common narrow-leaf sage is a hardy perennial that can be grown from seeds or plants.

▶ **Adaptability**
Sage is usually hardy in hardiness Zone 5 and south if given good drainage. I have seen sage on a hillock of heavy soil live into a second generation of gardeners.

▶ **How to plant**
Direct-seed sage from mid-spring to midsummer. Set out plants after spring frost danger is past.

▶ **Continuing care**
Sage plants should be cut back after blooming and before seeds form and slow down the formation of new shoots for harvest and drying. The foliage dries quickly and retains its color.

Culinary TIP

Sage has a pungent, musty taste that pairs best with pork, egg, bean, and cheese-based dishes, as well as in poultry dressings. Sage also freezes well; just pop it in an airtight bag and freeze for later use. Common, or 'Narrow-leaf gray', sage has the best flavor and aroma.

SUMMER SAVORY

Summer savory plants tuck in nicely between more substantial herbs and vegetables. You may find plants of winter savory, a perennial, sold alongside summer savory.

ESSENTIAL STATS

▶ **Grow from**
Summer savory, an annual, is usually started from direct-seeding. Because it does not produce vigorous growth, several plants are needed to produce enough shoots for drying. A dozen plants will supply two people. The plants are small at maturity; 12 can be grown in 3 feet of row. Winter savory, a perennial, is not used in cooking but makes a handsome edging for flower beds.

▶ **When to plant**
Plant in late spring and at monthly intervals through midsummer to maintain a fresh supply.

▶ **Continuing care**
The delicate-looking plants of summer savory need little care except for watering during dry spells. The plants may need staking for extra support. They flower and die off in late summer.

Culinary TIP

If you are attempting to add more vegetables to your diet, you'll appreciate how summer savory can enhance the taste of green beans and shelled beans. I also combine fresh savory with cilantro to flavor black or pinto beans cooked with bits of ham or bacon crumbles. Crush savory in your hand before use to release the flavor.

HOW I *Dry Herbs*

THE TRADITIONAL ADVICE FOR DRYING HERBS calls for hanging them upside down in a warm, dark, well-ventilated spot such as the one pictured below. **The combination of heat, dryness, and darkness maintains the color of the herbs.** My method involves large paper bags and the hot, dry, dark space behind the seats of my small pickup truck.

During the summer, I usually have several bags of different herbs standing open in my truck. When they have dried enough to feel crispy, I stuff them in labeled and dated gallon-size freezer bags, and then store them in a dark pantry, or any warm, dark room. I find it's best not to crush herbs until just prior to using them.

Of all the herbs, sweet basil is the most difficult to dry. It tends to turn black and lose much of its flavor without special handling. Nothing worked well enough until **I tried rolling a layer of freshly-cut basil between two large towels** and closing the ends of the roll with rubber bands. I leave the roll in a dark, dry room for about three days, then transfer the wilted but still green leaf terminals to large paper bags that I place in my truck. The limp leaves tend to pack into dense layers, so I fluff them whenever I run errands. After less than a week in the back of my truck, again out of direct sunlight, **the basil is completely dry and highly aromatic, and it has turned a beautiful, gray-green color.**

I WINCE WHENEVER A WRITER RHAPSODIZES about growing herbs indoors during the winter. **While it should work in Florida or California, the long, often cloudy, winter days elsewhere don't provide sun-loving herb plants adequate light for photosynthesis.** Consequently, they slowly decline. They are usually finished off by the warm, hyper-dry winter air in most homes. Elsewhere, you can keep herb plants alive indoors and even harvest a few leaves as late as Thanksgiving, given a sunny window, but even that is pushing your luck.

If you have a cool basement where you can maintain temperature levels of 60° to 65° F. during the day and 50 to 55° at night, you can grow a few kinds of herbs beneath fluorescent lights. **The tubes need to be lowered to no more than 6 inches above the tops of the plants and burned for 12 to 16 hours daily.** The low temperatures go well with the relatively low foot-candle output of fluorescent lights. Should you wish to grow basil, which needs warmer temperatures, you would need metal-halide lamps, which produce many more foot-candles of light and more heat than fluorescent lights.

Walter Chandoha is able to grow a few herb species indoors during the winter. His home dates back 200 years, and parts of it remain cool but above freezing during winter months. Within these areas he utilizes the sunny spots to keep herb plants alive.

TARRAGON

The culinary herb known as French tarragon (*Artemisia dracunculus*) is a cold-hardy perennial that lives well over winter. Like fennel, it is an anise-scented herb.

ESSENTIAL STATS

Adaptability
French tarragon is easy to grow in Zones 3 through 5. But it is unhappy in the heat; growing it becomes progressively more difficult as you go south in Zones 6 through 10, where it can produce a flush of spring growth and then go virtually dormant during hot weather.

Grow from
Potted plants produced from vegetative divisions. Seeds of French tarragon are unavailable, because it never flowers and sets seeds.

When to plant
Early spring, for harvest of sprigs in the first season.

How to plant
Tarragon requires moisture-retentive soil such as modified clay loam and full sun all day. Grow in a raised bed with other herbs, such as thyme. Tarragon is also an excellent container plant.

Continuing care
French tarragon grows vigorously during spring and fall but slows during the summer. After a few years, the roots may become congested. It is easy to propagate by digging, dividing, and replanting divisions of the entire dormant crown in early spring; rinse off the soil in order to see the growing points.

THYME

Although numerous named varieties of thyme are available, most cooks prefer common thyme (*Thymus vulgaris*) for its warm, spicy flavor.

ESSENTIAL STATS

Grow from
Named cultivars of thymes should be purchased as plants as they do not come true from seeds. Plant in sun or partial shade, in well-drained soil, or potting mix if in containers.

Continuing care
Thyme grows best in a rock garden or on top of a wall, where more vigorous herbs won't overwhelm it. You may also grow thyme in raised beds or containers, which makes harvesting easier.

Recommended cultivars
'English' thyme is a hardy perennial that is propagated by cuttings or divisions. It is regarded as one of the most versatile of the thymes. Green-leaved 'Lemon' thyme has a distinct lemon flavor and aroma, thus needs to be used with discretion. Some of the variegated thymes are also lemon flavored.

Culinary TIP

Thyme's strong, pungent flavor is best used with restraint. Most recipes require only one teaspoon. Thyme is one of the easiest herbs to dry, but the wiry stems should be removed before use. The numerous ornamental "creeping thymes" are rarely used in cooking.

Advances in Organic Food Gardening

During the past few years, we have witnessed a breathtaking number of new gardening discoveries, products, and processes. These are geared not only to devoted organic gardeners but also to traditional gardeners who are becoming increasingly reluctant to use chemical fertilizers and toxic pest controls around their homes.

Today, scientists are using microphotography and other sophisticated techniques to identify soil organisms and understand how they interact with one another to create healthy soil. As discussed in Chapter 3, "Understanding Your Soil," we have discovered that each species performs a small but vital role in this complex process. These micro- and macro-organisms build marvelous structures throughout the topsoil. The open spaces between these structures allow oxygen and water to pass through, which is vital to the health of the soil. This "mellow" soil attracts and sustains earthworms that tunnel through the top-

soil, moving partially digested organic matter into lower soil layers and creating additional passageways for oxygen and water.

It seems that almost every week, there is new information about this amazing world beneath our feet, and how it contributes to the food we eat. But before we talk about the exciting developments in gardening that are on the horizon, let's begin with an unorthodox idea that created a revolution among organic gardeners more than a half-century ago. I am referring to the "no-till method," which was introduced by gardening expert and author Ruth Stout in the early 1950s.

What Is No-Till Gardening?

Some people called Ruth Stout "The Mulch Queen," others, "The No-Dig Duchess." I will agree that she was a feisty lady with unusual ideas about how to grow food crops. Stout maintained that covering the entire surface of a food garden with multiple layers of newspapers, and then piling old hay, straw, lawn clippings, and dried leaves on top of that could, and—more importantly—*should*, replace traditional spading and raking.

Many proponents of organic gardening quickly jumped on the no-till bandwagon and helped to promote it long before anyone, Stout included, fully grasped how or why this unconventional way of growing food worked.

Fifty years ago, scientists were still just beginning to see what occurred in the soil on a microscopic level and to comprehend the environmental damage caused by tilling. What most gardeners could see was that the newsprint layers discouraged weed seeds from germinating. They noticed that the mulch layer reduced evaporation during dry spells and kept soil moisture at a consistent level. They confirmed that as additional layers of mulch were added over two or three layers of newsprint, few weed or grass seeds could sprout, and those that did were easy to remove. They could see vegetables and fruit growing to their full genetic potential.

In this no-till garden, newspaper and organic matter are piled on top of the soil to prevent weeds from sprouting.

My Experience

Prior to learning about Ruth Stout's no-till method, I had practiced only traditional tillage, turning over the soil with a spade in the spring and raking it into seedbeds. Her method made sense to me, and I decided to try it. At the time, we lived in a tiny tract house on the northwest side of Detroit. I enclosed the backyard with a low chain-link fence, creating a garden of 2,000 square feet.

In those days, I couldn't afford to buy topsoil, so I hauled black, sandy organic soil from a nearby creek bed using a small wheelbarrow. I had previously spaded the existing clay soil to remove stones and the roots of quack grass. I dumped the creek-bed soil atop the tilled soil and purchased straw from a feed and seed store. The fluffed straw covered the new topsoil about 6 inches deep. I followed Ruth Stout's directions for planting and maintaining a no-till garden for several years. Each year, my garden grew better and better crops, supplying plenty of fresh vegetables. I collected leaves and grass clippings that the neighbors had set out for garbage pickup and spread them atop newsprint over the decaying straw.

An autumn garden in the morning mist.

The no-till method is ideal for a small garden plot such as this raised bed. As the layers of organic matter decompose, the soil becomes more productive.

Backsliding

As I moved around the country, I tended 14 different gardens in 9 states, and at some point I abandoned the no-till method. I was not disenchanted with it, but my food gardens were shrinking in size and gaining in visibility. I found that it was more convenient to return to tillage and to grow food gardens that were "pretty" as well as productive. I must confess that I never again had gardens that grew and produced so abundantly, nor were they as free of insect damage.

I haven't owned a tiller in years because I prefer working the soil by hand. Each time I do, however, I wonder if I am damaging the soil, despite adding organic soil conditioner each time I turn it over. There is mounting evidence that even a single tillage to spade depth can damage soil microorganisms for years.

So I leave it to you to decide whether to follow the no-till method. I can assure you that it works well. Unless you live in the country, you won't be able to find spoiled hay or straw, and baled straw can be expensive. You can use clippings from turf not sprayed with herbicide. Another economical substitute for straw or hay would be twice-shredded municipal yard waste. Dressed atop dry leaves to keep them from blowing around, over layers of newsprint, you should be able to achieve results comparable to those using straw or hay mulch. When using municipal waste, scatter a generous application of organic fertilizer and lime (as needed) before applying the mulch.

An attractive mulch alternative would be shredded hardwood bark. You might need boards or edging to keep the mulch from drifting over exposed rows, and you would need bottomless tin cans around plants such as peppers to keep the mulch away from stems. Raised beds are difficult to maintain when mulching like this.

Just remember that mulches keep the soil temperature 5 to 10 degrees below that of soil exposed to the sun. Consequently, you should delay planting warm season vegetables by a week to 10 days after the average spring frost-free date.

What Is No-Till Gardening? 🌿 **165**

How To Manage A No-Till Food Garden

I f you cover the soil completely with newspapers and then place straw, old hay, dried leaves, or dried grass clippings on top, how do you plant seeds and set out plants? The process isn't that difficult. See "Planting Seeds," right, and "Setting Out Plants," opposite. If you have built up a 3- to 5-inch layer of mulch, you can walk on the planting area without compacting the soil below.

Grass mulch effectively supresses weed growth and eventually decomposes, adding more humus to the no-till garden.

■ **Using two stakes** and a cord or twine line, align the row where you want it. Poke both hands, fingers straight, down through all the layers, and gently pull them apart to expose a narrow row of soil, following the guide string.

■ **Make a shallow furrow** down the row; scatter seeds thinly; press them into the furrow; and cover them with a thin scattering of play sand. Label the row with the name of the variety and the date of seeding.

■ **When the seeds have germinated** and have grown large enough to tell the seedlings from the weeds, pull out the weeds and thin your seedlings on one pass.

■ **After two or three weeks,** thin again. When the plants have grown as large as a teacup, pull mulch up close to them to stifle weed growth.

SETTING OUT *Plants*

- **Mark the location** for each plant with a stake. Pull the mulch back from a space slightly larger than the root ball. Punch through the newspaper. Use a bulb planter to make holes for plants in small pots or a trowel to dig holes for larger plants. Hold the excavated soil temporarily in a bucket.

- **Toss ½ cup of organic fertilizer** in each planting hole, and mix it with the soil in the bottom. When planting tomato, pepper, or eggplant seedlings, incorporate pelletized dolomitic limestone to help prevent blossom-end rot.

- **Straighten out roots** of plants that may be spiraling around the pot. If a mat of roots has formed at the bottom, slice it off. Set the plant so that the top of the root ball is flush with the surface of the soil. If the pot is made of peat, snap off the rim that extends above the surface of the potting soil. This will keep the rim from acting like a wick and drying out the root ball.

- **Crumble a bit of the soil** in a bucket, and use it to fill in around the root ball.

- **If cutworms have been a problem** in the past, set a bottomless tin can over each seedling. Leave the cans in place until the central stems of plants have grown too hard and tough to attract cutworms. Pull mulch up around the can.

Organic Products For Fighting Pests & Diseases

Scientists are making huge strides in understanding life processes in the soil, the organisms that inhabit it, and what causes the outbreaks of pathogens that trigger plant diseases. Some of their discoveries are astonishing in their potential. Unfortunately, new organic products developed as a result of these discoveries are often slow to reach the home gardener, mostly because of the expense involved in funding their research, development, and marketing. Here are some of the things in the pipeline.

Plant disease and weed fighters

With the aid of electron microscopes, scientists are identifying and naming some of the thousands of species of microorganisms in soil. They are gaining a better understanding of their functions, how they interact with other micro and macroorganisms, and how to propagate beneficial species and apply them to garden soils.

A few universities are evaluating simple, "bland" compounds such as diluted bleach for controlling foliar diseases. But don't try using bleach in your garden without following qualified instructions for dilution and safe application.

Disease-fighting organisms. BioWorks, Inc., is one of the companies that is developing and marketing biological fungicides. Their products, which include Rootshield and Plantshield HC, contain beneficial fungi and bacteria that control plant diseases by "eating" harmful pythium, rhizoctonia, and fusarium pathogens. Because they are living organisms, these products are perishable and should be used soon after purchase.

Simple, relatively safe fungicides. Bioworks, Inc., also markets Milstop, which is an organic fungicide made from potassium bicarbonate, a benign compound. It kills the spores of powdery mildew, black spot of roses, and numerous other pathogens on contact by pulling water out of them. Early tests indicate that Milstop is harmless to many beneficial insects.

Fatty acid herbicides. Monterey Lawn and Garden Products, Inc., makes an herbicidal soap concentrate. Diluted as directed and sprayed on weeds, it kills all but the toughest kinds within four hours. It is made from a naturally occurring organic material. This and other organic items are available through large, independent garden centers.

Pest controls

The West Coast is a bit further along than the rest of the country in the availability of organically approved pest controls, especially beneficial insects and predatory microorganisms. Thankfully, most producers and distributors of these products invest a lot of money in research and development and are sure of the safety and efficacy of their products before they put them on the market.

Simple, relatively safe snail and slug bait. Monterey Lawn and Garden Products, Inc., manufactures Sluggo, which combines iron phosphate with a bait that attracts slugs and snails. It is safe to use around pets and wildlife and is replacing metaldehyde-based slug and snail baits, which can be harmful to pets.

Fermentation products. Monterey Garden Insect Spray can replace synthetic sprays that can be toxic to humans and pets. Its active ingredient is spinosad, a broad-spectrum insecticide made by fermenting certain soil microbes. Trials have proved that spinosad can control caterpillars, leafminers, thrips, borers, and more.

Botanical and biological insecticides. Neem oil, which is pressed from the seeds of a tree that is indigenous to

India, has been used to repel insects in North America for several years. It has been proved effective against numerous species of insects and mites, as well as certain foliar diseases. According to the Environmental Protection Agency, neem oil works by deterring the normal life cycle of certain insects, including feeding, molting, mating, and egg laying.

Harvesting abundant lettuce and kale.

Home gardeners can expect to see many safe and effective organic products on the market soon, left. The squash vine borers that killed this plant, as well as squash bugs, can be controlled by organic materials, above. A praying mantis egg case will soon hatch beneficial garden insects, below.

Beneficial insects for controlling aphids. We are now seeing beneficial insects, such as lady beetles and praying mantises, offered for home garden use. Several species are already being multiplied and sold to commercial vegetable growers and greenhouse operators. However, I feel that the greatest promise may be with predatory nematodes, which are microscopic, worm-like organisms that have an insatiable appetite for targeted pathogens. Several companies operate insectaries for producing beneficial insects and nematodes. Most of these specialists market primarily to organic farmers and fruit-tree orchards and secondarily to organic gardeners.

BIRDS, FINGERS, *and* GOOD BUGS

SOME YEARS BACK, when my kids were small, they were a big help in our food garden. **They planted, hoed, weeded, fetched, and ate while they picked—raspberries, strawberries, and cherry tomatoes.** But the activity they enjoyed most was picking—and squashing—bugs. They picked Japanese beetles and Colorado potato beetles and drowned them in jars of kerosene. They squashed the tiny, yellow clusters of Mexican bean-beetle eggs, and then wiped their fingers on their pants, vying with each other to see whose jeans were more yellow. It was okay with me because hand picking was, and still is, my preferred method of bug control.

Birds devour the bugs that picking and squashing miss. To attract them to the garden, we provide them with plenty of water for drinking and bathing. A row of conifers gives them a place to nest, roost, and hide from our many cats. As an added incentive, I scatter birdseed on the ground and keep the hanging feeders full.

I also get a big assist in bug control from praying mantises. To ensure their protection during the growing season, I collect their egg cases from the shrubs and trees around our farm in winter and early spring, and then place them throughout the garden. When the eggs hatch, hundreds of tiny mantises patrol the garden, eating aphids and flea beetles off the vegetables.

Still another helpful critter in the garden is the braconid wasp, which lays its eggs inside the tomato hornworm. So when you spy a fat, green worm covered with hundreds of tiny, white cocoons, let it be. The cocoons are feeding off the worm, which eventually dies. These cocoons hatch and become wasps. As the wasps multiply, you'll see fewer and fewer hornworms in your garden.

Green cabbageworms feed voraciously on the leaves of vegetables in the *Brassica* family, which includes cabbage, broccoli, Brussels sprouts, cauliflower, kale, and collards. One of the best ways to prevent them from devouring your crops is to **cover the young plants with Agronet, a floating row cover made from porous plastic.** This prevents the white cabbage butterfly from laying its eggs. If you don't use the covering, check your plants daily, and hand pick the worms. Better yet, get your kids to pick them! —*Walter Chandoha*

This potato beetle is about to be plucked and dispatched in kerosene, top. Birds are happy to live among the tomato plants because they offer a convenient supply of worms and insects, above.

Modern Victory Gardens

The First Family made an important statement about self-reliance, sustainability, and good nutrition when they planted a food garden on the White House lawn. Still, I wish I could convince our president to take an even bigger step and add food gardens for the hungry and homeless to his long list of urgent projects.

I would do this by asking a spokesperson for Feeding America, the national association of food banks, to update the president on how many people now depend on donated food, and how many more there are likely to be in the future.

More than 25 million people turn to food banks and soup kitchens for groceries and hot meals each year. Most of them are average families who are accustomed to being self-sufficient. But without jobs and unable to make their house payments, they are forced to seek food and shelter wherever they can. Unfortunately, regional food banks and local food pantries don't have enough supplies to meet the demand. Charitable contributions have dropped off, and corporations that once gave generous financial support are being forced to cut back.

This shortage of healthy food is not new to our

country. When President Roosevelt grappled with the challenge of feeding our troops during WWII, he called a small group of gardening experts to the nation's capital to assist him. Out of these meetings, the Victory Garden concept was born. FDR threw the weight of his considerable popularity behind the Victory Garden movement (as did his wife, Eleanor), and within two years, Americans grew enough of their own food to free up thousands of tons of fresh and canned produce for our troops.

I believe we now need a multifaceted Victory Garden program to provide ample nutritious food to the hungry in our communities. While local agencies are set up to distribute fresh produce, they simply aren't getting enough. Indeed, many needy families who rely on food assistance must make do with cans and packages of highly processed, high-calorie food.

How Can We Help?

The most obvious solution is for everyone to pitch in and grow enough food to share with their neighbors in need. But despite my affection for homegrown produce, I would place home gardens in third place, behind local farms and "caring gardens," which are plots established on the grounds of churches and schools, as a source of fresh food for the hungry.

Cities also need to organize corps of retired people, young enough to supply the stamina for gardening, to put vacant urban land to work growing food for delivery to food banks and pantries. They also need to enlist the aid of trained volunteers for planning and supervising the logistics. These include Master Gardeners, who have been certified through the Extension Services of agricultural colleges, and community garden administrators.

VEGETABLES & HERBS *for a Caring Garden*

- Basil
- Beets
- Broccoli
- Brussels sprouts
- Bush beans
- Carrots
- Chives
- Cilantro
- Cucumbers
- Dill
- Eggplant
- Lettuce
- Melons
- Onion
- Oregano
- Parsley
- Peas
- Peppers
- Potatoes
- Radishes
- Spinach
- Summer squash
- Sweet corn
- Swiss chard
- Thyme
- Tomatoes

Local Farmers

Local market growers already have the infrastructure needed to produce healthy food and get it to consumers quickly. We can encourage these farmers to set aside special plots to be harvested by volunteers and delivered to food banks and pantries.

The problem is that many of these growers lack the funding necessary for such an expansion. But with the help of federal or state loans, they could purchase small, efficient greenhouses, which would help them to extend their growing seasons and produce more food to sell. They would be given government loans for crops donated to food banks, with the value of the crop based on prevailing prices at the time of the donation. Hopefully, this plan would encourage growers to plant special plots of staple vegetables—such as greens, potatoes, sweet potatoes, onions, and winter squash—and deliver the entire crop to a local food bank.

Fresh beans are at the top of the list of welcome contributions to a regional food bank or community food pantry.

Learning the facts about growing cabbage.

Caring Gardens

In a caring garden, volunteers work together to grow vegetables on a sizable plot of land and donate most or all they produce to a local food bank or pantry. One such program in North America, Plant A Row for the Hungry (PAR), has been racking up impressive contributions from plots of 5,000 to 10,000 square feet. Home gardeners with large vegetable plots also contribute to the PAR program.

But more caring gardens are desperately needed. They can be established quickly on the grounds of houses of worship and schools and, with proper management, can produce significant crops for delivery to food banks and pantries. In fact, in the first full season of operation, they can return four to five times the investment in soil preparation, seeds, plants, and water.

If you are a member of a church, synagogue, mosque, or school with suitable land, you might want to organize a group of volunteers to build a caring garden. The information in Chapter 2, "Where and How Does Your Garden Grow," is useful for getting started.

At this caring garden, a young helper picks vine-ripened plum tomatoes for distribution to a community food pantry.

A shady spot provides a respite from the hot sun.

CHECKLIST FOR A
Successful Caring Garden

■ **Full sun.** Ideal for plants, but a small shade structure over a picnic table and benches would be greatly appreciated by volunteer gardeners.

■ **Pest control.** You can imagine the dismay of volunteer gardeners if even one deer, groundhog, or armadillo destroys a row of vegetables. Tall plastic-net fencing keeps out deer, and a fence made of 1-inch mesh chicken wire that is 3 feet high and buried to a 1-foot depth discourages burrowing pests.

■ **Water.** A single faucet can serve a 5,000-square-foot garden, but two are much better. Two faucets with "Y" adapters can handle four hoses, or soaker hoses laid down the center of raised beds.

■ **Two 2-gallon pump sprayers.** One is for insecticides and the other for fatty-acid herbicides. (See "Preparing Your First Garden Plot" on page 30.)

■ **A large table with back and side splash guards.** This is for washing vegetables. It should be constructed of sealed wood. The top should be shaped like a funnel at one end to capture wash water for re-use in the garden. A shallow livestock-watering trough raised on a frame might do an even better job. You will need another station for draining washed vegetables.

■ **A prefabricated wooden shed.** For storing tools, pest controls, fertilizer, pots, and other essential gardening items. Sheds made of plastic are more vulnerable to break ins. It should be equipped with a sturdy lock. A volunteer who lives nearby should be assigned to opening and closing the garden and the tool shed daily.

■ **A sign that reads:** "These vegetables are being grown for delivery to the [name of food bank or pantry] to feed the needy. If you see anyone in the garden who is not wearing a volunteer badge, please phone [number of the sponsoring institution]."

■ **Clip-on plastic badges** reading "Volunteer Gardener" and the name of your institution. Keep badges in a basket in the tool shed, and ask that they be returned at the end of the day.

A caring garden is a labor of love.

Community Gardens

Although both caring gardens and community gardens generate wholesome, locally grown produce, in community gardens, volunteers traditionally grow food for their own use and enjoyment.

Community gardening is a well-established institution in Europe. In Holland and Denmark, where open land is scarce, odd corners and narrow strips between buildings are leased to home gardeners. Typically, these small plots are passed on to children or close friends.

Community gardening in America dates back to the early twentieth century. In New York City, many neighborhood residents rely on community gardens, not only for fresh produce, but also for the green space, social activity, and sense of purpose that these gardens provide. Metropolitan Los Angeles has long had more community gardens than any other western city. Often, these inner-city gardens are sandwiched into small, landlocked spaces abutting freeway overpasses.

These unsettled economic times have injected a sense of urgency and purpose into community gardening. In my own town, University of Missouri specialists are cooperating with volunteers and local businesses in a program called "Grow Healthy, Columbia." Community gardens and sharing gardens are part of its plan to provide more and better food for low-income families. At the CASA community garden in Huntsville, Alabama, the volunteers—members of local civic and church groups—grow produce and donate it to housebound elderly folk who live in subsidized housing. In 2000, the group donated more than 18,000 pounds of produce to 7,000 needy folks. I watched one garden, which went on to win a national award, develop in Spartanburg, South Carolina. It was planted and tended by a local chapter of Master Gardeners with advice from experts at Clemson University. The Master Gardeners grew and donated 14,000 pounds of produce in a single season. They also worked with local market growers to gather leftover produce after the harvest.

A community garden in New York City flourishes in an empty lot, above. Community gardening has a long tradition in Europe. This plot in Italy is tended with care by its owner, below.

GARDEN *Gurus*

THE REALLY FORTUNATE COMMUNITY GARDENS attract one or two **experienced members who informally mentor first-timers and teach sound practices by personal example.** Many years ago, I visited a big community garden in Dayton, Ohio. The "star" among the dozens of gardeners was a small, wizened gentleman from the Philippines. He couldn't speak English well, but could he grow vegetables! These included not only the familiar kinds but many tropical varieties, which was quite an accomplishment given the area's relatively short summers.

It is never too early to teach children how to grow—and share—good food.

Finding or Starting a Community Garden

If you would like to become involved in a community gardening project, your local parks and recreation departments can help you find one in your locale. You can also contact the American Community Gardening Association (info@communitygarden.org), or visit its Web site at communitygarden.org, where you will find a national database of community gardens.

The ACG Web site also contains detailed information and practical advice on starting up a community garden. If you choose this route, you'll need to work with your town or city to find available land, such as at a church or school. Keep in mind that the owner of the property must agree to give you long-term use of the land. Shutting down a thriving community garden to expand a parking lot or to erect a building can cause shock waves of resentment and disappointment.

Once you organize a group, logistics, such as the annual fee for leasing a plot, buying soil amendments and other materials, dividing chores, settling disputes, and the like, must be decided and set in advance. Try to persuade local merchants and civic groups to contribute items such as fencing and gravel for access driveways. Establish open days and hours for the garden, and assign the task of opening and closing the locked gate to a person who lives nearby.

How Large are Community Gardens, and Who Manages Them?

Most community gardens are at least ¼ acre in size. Any smaller than that makes it difficult to justify a coordinator and startup costs. Typically, the garden has access to running water and is fenced and locked at night for protection from vandals. Larger gardens have full- or part-time managers who assign plots, offer advice, settle disputes, and order soil amendments.

Community gardens are usually divided into plots of approximately 200 square feet each. Gardeners often work their way up to farming multiple plots as they gain experience and confidence. Some older community gardens resemble a collection of small outdoor living rooms, each with a gate opening to an access road. Some of the plots are tastefully landscaped with ornamentals, even water features. Others are straightforward food plots, with just enough flowers to provide a few blooms for bouquets.

This large, well-established urban garden has the benefit of a manager who handles most of the organizational details.

Members enjoy sharing and swapping produce.

THE CASE FOR
Suburban Community Gardens

IN URBAN AREAS, the appeal of a living, growing patch of green is obvious. **But why bother with a community garden if you've got your own backyard?** Community gardens within suburban neighborhoods often attract gardeners who have land around their homes, but not enough for large, spreading kinds of vegetables. So they grow sweet corn, squash, cucumbers, and potatoes in a community garden plot and tomatoes, peppers, salad greens, and herbs on their home grounds. **Most community gardeners value the fellowship of fellow gardeners and the good-natured bragging and sharing that goes on.** Community gardens break through the isolation that develops in the suburbs, where homes can become islands of loneliness.

As our population ages, we can expect more retirees to join the ranks of volunteer gardeners working to feed the hungry.

Youthful volunteers tend a garden in Manhattan.

The Future of Community Gardening

Research indicates that gardeners are planting more vegetables and small fruit every year. With more people living in apartments and condos and fewer in homes with enough land to accommodate a garden, it follows that more families will be seeking plots for growing some of their own food. The price of gasoline may rise again, which will persuade more people to look for recreation closer to home. As our population ages, more retirees will join the ranks of community gardeners, and they'll come to appreciate the sense of community that can develop as they share tips and swap produce with fellow gardeners.

Finally, as we continue to seek solutions for feeding our country's hungry and homeless, more members of religious and civic groups are likely to take action, securing land and planting crops that will be delivered to local food banks.

Zone Maps

Hardiness

Plants thrive in an environment that approximates their native habitat. For many years, plants have been labeled with their USDA (United States Department of Agriculture) hardiness zone rating, which indicates their tolerance to cold. Many of the plants listed in this book are labeled with their USDA Hardiness Zone rating.

Although the USDA ratings are a good starting point, several factors can affect their accuracy. For example, city temperatures tend to be 5° to 10°F warmer than those of the surrounding countryside, raising the hardiness rating of a city garden by a full zone.

Every garden has microclimates that may be warmer or cooler or drier or more humid. The longer you garden in one location, the more familiar you will become with its microclimates. A hardiness rating of "Zones 4 or 5–7 or 8," suggests that the plant may survive the winter cold with protection in the warmer parts of Zone 4, but is safer in Zone 5. That same plant may need shade to protect it from the sun's heat in Zone 8, but it is more likely to thrive in Zone 7. A plant that is surviving, but not thriving, is under stress and therefore more vulnerable to pests and diseases. Don't be dissuaded from growing a plant at the extremes of its stated cold tolerance. But be prepared to give that plant more attention.

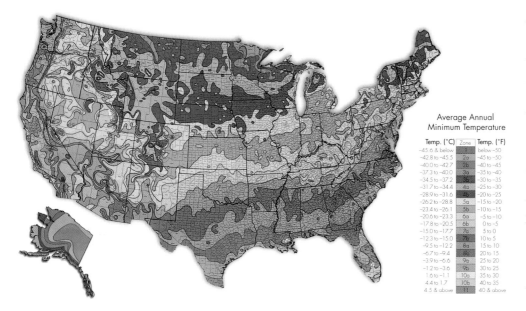

Average Annual
Minimum Temperature

Temp. (°C)	Zone	Temp. (°F)
-45.6 & below	1	below -50
-42.8 to -45.5	2a	-45 to -50
-40.0 to -42.7	2b	-40 to -45
-37.3 to -40.0	3a	-35 to -40
-34.5 to -37.2	3b	-30 to -35
-31.7 to -34.4	4a	-25 to -30
-28.9 to -31.6	4b	-20 to -25
-26.2 to -28.8	5a	-15 to -20
-23.4 to -26.1	5b	-10 to -15
-20.6 to -23.3	6a	-5 to -10
-17.8 to -20.5	6b	0 to -5
-15.0 to -17.7	7a	5 to 0
-12.3 to -15.0	7b	10 to 5
-9.5 to -12.2	8a	15 to 10
-6.7 to -9.4	8b	20 to 15
-3.9 to -6.6	9a	25 to 20
-1.2 to -3.6	9b	30 to 25
1.6 to -1.1	10a	35 to 30
4.4 to 1.7	10b	40 to 35
4.5 & above	11	40 & above

THE USDA HARDINESS MAP divides North America into 11 zones according to average minimum winter temperatures. Hardiness zones are used to identify regions to which plants are suited based on their cold tolerance, which is what "hardiness" means. Many factors, such as elevation and moisture level, come into play when determining whether a plant is suitable for your region. Local climates may vary from what is shown on this map. Contact your local Cooperative Extension Service for recommendations for your area.

CANADA'S PLANT HARDINESS ZONE MAP outlines the different zones in Canada where various types of vegetables, fruits, and herbs will most likely survive. It is based on the average climatic conditions of each area. The hardiness map is divided into nine major zones: the harshest is 0 and the mildest is 8. Relatively few plants are suited to zone 0. Subzones (e.g., 4a or 4b, 5a or 5b) are also noted in the map legend. These subzones are most familiar to Canadian gardeners. Some significant local factors, such as micro-topography, amount of shelter, and subtle local variations in snow cover, are too small to be captured on the map. Year-to-year variations in weather and gardening techniques can also have a significant impact on plant survival in any particular location.

Plant Hardiness Zones

0a	4a
0b	4b
1a	5a
1b	5b
2a	6a
2b	6b
3a	7a
3b	7b
	8a

Heat Tolerance

Researchers have recently discovered that plants begin to suffer cellular damage at temperatures over 86°F (30°C). The American Horticultural Society's Heat-Zone Map divides the country into 12 zones, based on the average number of days each year that a given region experiences "heat days," or temperatures over 86°F. The zones range from Zone 1 (no heat days) to Zone 12 (210 heat days).

In the near future, plants will be labeled with four numbers to indicate cold hardiness and heat tolerance. For example, a tulip may be 3–8, 8–1. If you live in USDA Zone 7 and AHS Zone 7, this label indicates that you can leave tulips outside in your garden all year.

It will take several years for most garden plants to be labeled reliably for heat tolerance. Unusual seasons with fewer or more hot days than normal will invariably affect results. The AHS Heat-Zone ratings assume that adequate water is supplied to the roots of the plant at all times. The accuracy of the coding can be substantially distorted by a lack of water, even for a brief period in the life of the plant.

Both the Cold-Hardiness Zone Map and the Heat-Zone Map are tools to help you get started on creating gardens and landscapes. After growing plants in one place for several years, you will become the expert and come to know what plants you can and cannot successfully grow.

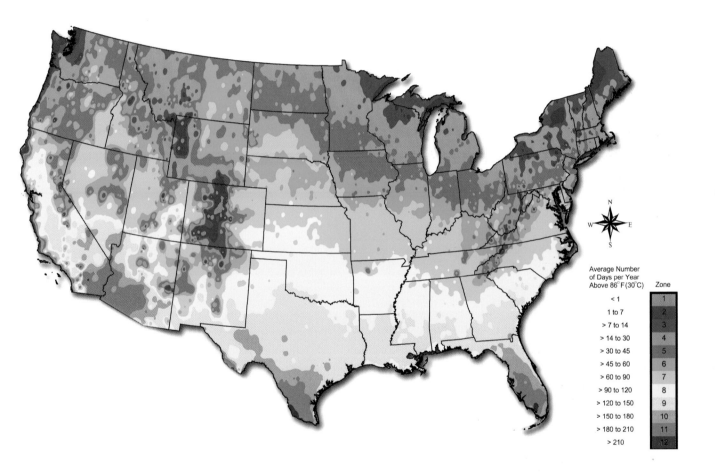

Average Number of Days per Year Above 86° F (30°C)	Zone
< 1	1
1 to 7	2
> 7 to 14	3
> 14 to 30	4
> 30 to 45	5
> 45 to 60	6
> 60 to 90	7
> 90 to 120	8
> 120 to 150	9
> 150 to 180	10
> 180 to 210	11
> 210	12

THE AMERICAN HORTICULTURAL SOCIETY HEAT-ZONE MAP divides the United States into 12 zones based on the average annual number of days a region's temperatures climb above 86°F (30°C), the temperature at which the cellular proteins of plants begin to experience injury. Introduced in 1998, the AHS Heat-Zone Map holds significance, especially for gardeners in southern and transitional zones. Nurseries, growers, and other plant sources will gradually begin listing both cold hardiness and heat tolerance zones for plants, including grass plants. Using the USDA Plant Hardiness map, which can help determine a plant's cold tolerance, and the AHS Heat-Zone Map, gardeners will be able to safely choose plants that tolerate their region's lowest and highest temperatures.

Glossary

Acidic. Soil with a low pH, below 7.0, and unsuitable for plants that prefer alkaline soil.

Alkaline. Soil with a high pH, above 7.0, also called lime soil, and unsuitable for plants that prefer a neutral or acidic soil.

Annual. A plant that grows from a seed and flowers in the same year; most vegetables are annuals.

Bare-Root. Plants that have been grown in the soil, then lifted out of it and sold to gardeners without being planted in pots.

Bacillus thuringiensis (BT). A naturally occurring bacteria that is lethal to caterpillars but harmless to other animals and most insects. It is sold as a soluble powder to kill caterpillar pests.

Balanced Fertilizer. A fertilizer with equal parts of the three main nutrients needed by plants: nitrogen, phosphorus, and potassium.

Beneficial Nematodes. Minute worms that can be purchased and spread on the soil to kill pests.

Biennial. A plant that produces a storage root in its first year and flowers in the second year; most root crops are biennials.

Blanch. To cover plants to exclude light and make the leaves or hearts pale and milder in taste.

Bolting. When a plant sends up a flower stalk early due to unfavorable growing conditions. See also "interruption to growth."

Brassica. The family of plants that includes cabbage and its many edible relatives, from turnips to cauliflowers.

Broadcast. To scatter seeds in patches rather than along single rows to produce a mass of leaves, a technique useful for salad greens.

Canker. A dead spot on a plant stem resulting from a disease caused by a fungus or bacterium.

Cloche. A temporary transparent cover for individual plants to protect them from cold weather, also known as a "hot cap."

Cold Frame. An outdoor, boxlike structure with a plastic or glass top similar to a window that is used for starting seeds and protecting young plants in cold weather.

Compost. Dead plant matter collected into a pile that decomposes; it produces a useful material, called humus, that can be used as a mulch or as a soil additive.

Cover Crop. A crop grown not to eat but to cover bare soil and to provide nutrients to the soil; see also "green manure."

Crop Rotation. A method of preventing pests and diseases by moving crops to a different part of the vegetable garden year to year in a set sequence.

Cross-Pollination. Fertilization by transfer of pollen from the anthers of one flower to the stigma of another.

Cultivar. A named form of a fruit or vegetable that is guaranteed to be distinct from other varieties and conforms to a description; the name is usually enclosed in single quotes.

Cut-and-Come-Again. A technique of cutting salad greens so that the plants resprout to provide a second and third crop of leaves.

Determinate. Plants, such as tomatoes, that grow to a set height and produce most of their fruit at the same time; see also "indeterminate."

Direct-Seeding. Sowing seeds directly in the soil where they are to grow, rather than transplanting seedlings.

Division. A section of a perennial plant that has been pulled or cut away from a mature plant; this technique can be used to increase several perennial herbs.

Dormant. The state of a plant when it is alive but not actively growing. Plants may be dormant when conditions are

not suitable—for example, during winter when the temperature is cold.

Draw Hoe. A hoe with the blade at right angles to the handle, which is pulled toward you to remove weeds.

Early. Varieties of fruit or vegetables that grow faster than other varieties; see also "main crop."

F1 Hybrid. Seeds produced by crossing two specific parent types; hybrid varieties produce plants that are vigorous and almost identical to each other.

Fertilizer. Any product containing a concentrated form of nutrients that plants need to grow. Fertilizers can contain man-made chemicals or products of natural origin—the latter is an organic fertilizer.

Floating Row Cover. A translucent material made from spun plastic that can be used to cover crops, keeping them warm while letting air and rain through; it also keeps insect pests out.

Force. To cover crops before they start into normal growth to produce pale tender leaves or hearts.

Fungicide. A chemical or natural product used to kill or prevent diseases caused by fungi.

Furrow. A narrow, shallow trench made in the soil so that seeds are buried at the correct depth and in straight lines.

Green Manure. A cover crop grown especially to dig into the soil to help add organic matter.

Handpick. To remove insects or other small garden pests from plants by picking them off manually.

Hand Pull. Removing weed seedlings by hand from among rows of crops, where a hoe cannot be used.

Harden Off. To get plants that were started off indoors used to being outdoors by leaving them outside for longer each day over a period of a week or so.

Hardpan. A layer of hard soil beneath the surface often caused by repeatedly cultivating to the same depth. It can lead to poor drainage and poor root growth.

Hardy. Describing a plant that is more tolerant of cold weather; some can survive frosts.

Heirloom Variety. An open-pollinated plant that has been around for a long time, usually from before 1940, sometimes kept going by gardening enthusiasts.

Herbicide. A chemical for killing weeds.

Hilling. A technique in which seeds are planted in a small hill, or mound, of soil, usually about 12 inches (30cm) high, or the technique of pulling soil up around the plant as it grows. This hill protects the neck of these plants, which are susceptible to rotting.

Horticultural Oil. A solution of natural oils used to kill insect pests and acceptable to organic gardeners.

Humus. The component of soil that consists of partially decomposed organic matter.

Indeterminate. Plants, especially tomatoes, that continue to grow from the top and produce fruit right through the summer; see also "determinate."

Insecticidal Soap. A natural product used to kill insect pests and that is acceptable to organic gardeners.

Insecticide. A chemical for killing insect pests. Most are developed from man-made chemicals, but some are produced from naturally occurring chemicals, suitable for organic gardening.

Interplanting. A system of planting two or more crops in the same field, either mixed together or in alternating rows.

Interruption to Growth. A setback to a plant due to drought, cold, or heat, which stops it from growing or makes it flower early; see also "bolting."

Leaf Mold. A compost made from leaves collected in the fall; these rot slowly, so they are often kept separate from other garden waste in the compost pile.

Legume. A family of plants that includes peas and beans; all have the ability to turn nitrogen in the air into nitrogen salts they can use as food.

Loam. A soil that contains a fertile mixture of sand, clay, and silt.

Main Crop. Varieties of fruit or vegetables that are ready for harvesting within the main bearing period; early or late varieties bear outside this period.

Milky Spore Disease. A solution of a natural bacteria that kills the grubs of Japanese beetles.

Mulch. A layer of material laid over the surface of the soil to retain moisture, prevent weeds, or protect it from cold, heat, and wind. It may be organic, such as compost, or inorganic, such as a plastic sheet.

Nematodes. Minute worms that are abundant in the soil. Although they are mostly harmless, there are a few that can harm garden plants.

No-Till. A method of managing a vegetable garden that relies on adding organic mulch each year to improve the soil, instead of digging.

NPK. The ratio of the main plant nutrients in a fertilizer—nitrogen, potash, and phosphate—and given on the package in percentages, such as 7:7:7.

Open-Pollinated. Seeds collected from plants that have been pollinated naturally; seeds of open-pollinated varieties produce plants that are all slightly different from their parents.

Organic. Anything that is of plant or animal origin; also used to describe a way of gardening that uses only natural materials.

Organic Matter. Bulky material, such as manure or garden compost, that is used to improve soil and help feed plants.

Overwinter. To keep plants growing through the winter to crop in the following spring; also refers to when insects and other creatures survive outdoors during the winter.

Peat Moss. Decomposed sphagnum moss that is mixed with garden soil to improve its condition and to add organic matter.

Perennial. A plant that keeps growing for years, flowering each year, such as most fruit and some herbs and vegetables.

Pesticide. Any chemical used to kill pests, sometimes used as a general term to include fungicides and herbicides, too.

Petiole. The stalk that joins the leaf of a plant to its stem.

pH. The measure of whether a soil is acidic or alkaline. A pH of 7.0 is neutral, higher than this is alkaline and lower is acidic.

Push Hoe. A hoe with a flat blade that extends from the end of the handle. It is pushed away from you to remove weeds.

Raised Bed. A garden structure built on top of native soil and piled with several inches of soil and amendments.

Repot. To move a seedling or a started plant into a larger pot.

Root Nodule. Lumps on the roots of peas and beans that convert nitrogen in the air into food.

Seed Starter Tray. A plastic tray divided into several square divisions; a seed sown in each will produce an easily separated seedling to plant outdoors.

Set. Started onion bulbs ready to grow into mature plants as an alternative to growing from seeds.

Side-Dress. To scatter fertilizer along a row of half-grown vegetables to boost its yield.

Slow Release. A fertilizer that is made to release its nutrients over a period of weeks or months instead of all at once.

Started Plant. Plants grown from seeds in divided trays and available from garden centers when ready to plant outdoors.

Succession Planting. Sowing seeds for a new crop as soon as one is harvested to ensure the most efficient use of the garden space.

Tender. A plant that does not survive cold conditions or frosts.

Thinning. The act of removing extra seedlings from a row to provide sufficient growing space for the remaining plants.

Tilth. The condition of the soil after it has been broken down and raked to create a fine, crumbly texture suitable for planting seeds.

Top-Dress. Scattering fertilizer over the soil before sowing a crop; it does not need to be mixed in.

Transplant. A young plant grown from a seed in a pot to be planted outside when conditions are suitable; also the act of planting out started plants.

Variety. See cultivar.

Resources

The resources on these pages are intended as supplemental information and are not a listing of the products and manufacturers represented by the photographs in this book.

Vegetable Seeds and Plants

Baker Creek Heirloom Seeds
2278 Baker Creek Rd.
Mansfield, MO 65704
(417) 924-8917
rareseeds.com
Specializes in rare and heirloom varieties.

W. Atlee Burpee Co.
300 Park Ave.
Warminster, PA 18974
(800) 333-5808
burpee.com
Large selection of seeds and plants.

The Cook's Garden
P.O. Box C5030
Warminster, PA 18974
(800) 457-9703
cooksgarden.com
Specializes in gourmet vegetables.

Dixondale Farms
P.O. Box 129
Carrizo Springs, TX 78834
(877) 367-1015
dixondalefarms.com
Specializes in onion plants.

Dominion Seed House
Box 2500
Georgetown, Ont. L7G 5LS
Canada
(800) 784-3037
dominion-seed-house.com
Serves Canadian growers.

Gourmet Seed International
HC12, Box 510
Tatum, NM 88267-9700
(575) 398-6111
gourmetseed.com
Specializes in international vegetable varieties.

Gurney Seed & Nursery Co.
P.O. Box 4178
Greendale, IN 47025-4178
(513) 354-1491
gurneys.com
Large selection of seeds and plants.

Harris Seeds
355 Paul Rd.
Rochester, NY 14624
(800) 544-7938
harrisseeds.com

Ed Hume Seeds, Inc.
P.O. Box 73160
Puyallup, WA 98375
humeseeds.com
Specializes in seeds for short growing seasons and cool climates.

Johnny's Selected Seeds
955 Benton Ave.
Winslow, ME 04901
(877) 564-6697
johnnyseeds.com
Employee-owned seed company.

J.W. Jung Seed Co.
335 S. High St.
Randolph, WI 53957-4162
(800) 297-3123
jungseed.com

Earl May Seed and Nursery Co.
208 N. Elm St.
Shenandoah, IA 51603-1339
earlmay.com

Nichols Garden Nursery
1190 Old Salem Rd. NE
Albany, OR 97321
(800) 422-3985
nicholsgardennursery.com
Specializes in herbs and rare seeds.

Page's Seeds
P.O. Box 158
Greene, NY 13778
(607) 656-4107
pageseed.com

Geo. W. Park Seed Co., Inc.
1 Parkton Ave.
Greenwood, S.C. 29647
(800) 213-0076
parkseed.com

Pinetree Garden Seeds
P.O. Box 300
New Gloucester, ME 04260
(207) 926-3400
superseeds.com

Renee's Garden
(formerly Shepherd's Seeds)
7389 W. Zayante Rd.
Felton, CA 95018
(888) 880-7228
reneesgarden.com
Specializes in gourmet vegetables and herbs.

Seed Savers Exchange
3994 N. Winn Rd.
Decorah, IA 56101
(563) 382-5990
seedsavers.org
Nonprofit organization for saving and sharing heirloom seeds.

Seeds of Change
(888) 762-7333
seedsofchange.com
Specializes in certified organic seeds and plants.

R.H. Shumway's
334 W Stroud St.
Randolph, WI. 53957-4162
(800) 342-9461
rhshumway.com

Stokes Seeds, Inc.
P.O. Box 538
Buffalo, NY 14240-0548
(800) 396-9238
stokeseeds.com

Territorial Seed Company
P.O. Box 158
Cottage Grove, OR 97424
(800) 626-0866
territorialseed.com

Thompson & Morgan
220 Faraday Ave.
Jackson, NJ 08527-5073
(800) 274-7333
tmseeds.com
Specializes in English seeds.

Tomato Growers Supply Co.
P.O. Box 60015
Fort Myers, FL 33906
(888) 478-7333
tomatogrowers.com
Offers more than 500 varieties of tomato and pepper seeds.

Totally Tomatoes
334 West Stroud St.
Randolph, WI 53956
(800) 345-5977
totallytomato.com

Vermont Bean Seed Co.
Garden Ln.
Bomoseen, VT 05732-0308
(800) 349-1071
vermontbean.com

Vesey's Seeds, Ltd.
P.O. Box 9000
Calais, ME 04619
(800) 363-7333
veseys.com

Willhite Seed, Inc.
P.O. Box 23
Poolville, TX 76487
(800) 828-1840
willhiteseed.com
Primarily seeds of melons.

Small Fruit and Berry Plants

Aaron's Nursery
P.O. Box 800
Sumner, GA 31789
(229) 556-9888.
aaronsfarm.com

Adams County Nursery
26 Nursery Rd.
P.O. Box 108
Aspers, PA 17304
(717) 677-8105
acnursery.com

Fruit-tree.com Nursery
19132 S.W. Neugebauer Rd.
Hillsboro, OR 97123-9464
fruit-tree.com

Heartland Blueberries
3704 New Jackson Hwy.
Hodgenville, KY 42748
(270) 766-2574
heartlandblueberries.com

Johnson Nursery
1352 Big Creek Rd.
Elijay, GA 30536
(888) 276-3187
johnsonnursery.com

Miller Nurseries
5060 W. Lake Rd.
Canandaigua, NY 14424
(800) 836-9630
millernurseries.com

Raintree Nursery
391 Butts Rd.
Morton, WA 98356
(360) 496-6400
raintreenursery.com

Van Well Nursery
P.O. Box 1339
Wenatchee, WA 98807
vanwell@vanwell.com
(800) 572-1553
vanwell.net

Waters Blueberry Farm
925 Bainbridge Rd.
Smithville, MO 64089
(816) 718-5948
watersblueberryfarm.com

Gardening Products

BioWorks, Inc.,
100 Rawson Rd. Ste. 205
Victor, NY 14564
(800) 877-9443
bioworksinc.com
Manufacturer of biofungicides.

Gardens Alive!
51 Schenley Pl.
Lawrenceberg, IN 47025
(513) 354-1482
gardensalive.com
Online retailer of environmentally-responsible gardening products.

Monterey Lawn and Garden Products, Inc.
P.O. Box 35000
Fresno, CA 93745-5000
(559) 499-2100
montereylawngarden.com
Manufactures and retails organic lawn and garden products.

Associations

American Community Gardening Association (ACGA)
1777 E. Broad St.,
Columbus, OH 43203-2040
(877) ASK-ACGA
communitygarden.org
Organization of volunteers and supporters of urban and rural community gardening in the U.S. and Canada.

Feeding America
35 E. Wacker Dr., Ste. 2000
Chicago, IL 60601
(800) 771-2303
feedingamerica.org
The largest domestic hunger-relief charity in the U.S.

Garden Writers Association
10210 Leatherleaf Ct.
Manassas, VA 20111
(703) 257-1032
gardenwriters.org
Founder and administrator of the Plant a Row for the Hungry (PAR) program.

Index

Photo Credits

All photography by Walter Chandoha, except as noted.

page 5: Kendra Martin
page 40: *bottom* Lee Foster/Bruce Coleman/Photoshot
page 42: *top* Dr. Jeremy Burgess/Science Library/Photo Researchers; *bottom sequence* Carl Weese/Joe Provey
page 43: *top* J. P. Ferrero/Jacana/Photo Researchers
page 119: *bottom* Teresa Azevedo/Dreamstime.com
page 120: *top* Lepas/Dreamstime.com
page 142: *top* Olga Lupol/Dreamstime.com
page 143: *top left* Edyta Pawlowska/Dreamstime.com; *top right* Tatjana Keisa/Dreamstime.com; *bottom right* Victorpr/Dreamstime.com; *bottom left* Anne Power/Dreamstime.com
page 153: *bottom* Guodingping/Dreamstime.com

Metric Equivalents

All measurements in this book are given in U.S. Customary units. If you wish to find metric equivalents, use the following tables and conversion factors.

Inches to Millimeters and Centimeters

1 in = 25.4 mm = 2.54 cm

in	mm	cm
1/16	1.5875	0.1588
1/8	3.1750	0.3175
1/4	6.3500	0.6350
3/8	9.5250	0.9525
1/2	12.7000	1.2700
5/8	15.8750	1.5875
3/4	19.0500	1.9050
7/8	22.2250	2.2225
1	25.4000	2.5400

Inches to Centimeters and Meters

1 in = 2.54 cm = 0.0254 m

in	cm	m
1	2.54	0.0254
2	5.08	0.0508
3	7.62	0.0762
4	10.16	0.1016
5	12.70	0.1270
6	15.24	0.1524
7	17.78	0.1778
8	20.32	0.2032
9	22.86	0.2286
10	25.40	0.2540
11	27.94	0.2794
12	30.48	0.3048

Feet to Meters

1 ft = 0.3048 m

ft	m
1	0.3048
5	1.5240
10	3.0480
25	7.6200
50	15.2400
100	30.4800

Square Feet to Square Meters

1 ft^2 = 0.092 903 04 m^2

Acres to Square Meters

1 acre = 4046.85642 m^2

Cubic Yards to Cubic Meters

1 yd^3 = 0.764 555 m^3

Ounces and Pounds (Avoirdupois) to Grams

1 oz = 28.349 523 g
1 lb = 453.5924 g

Pounds to Kilograms

1 lb = 0.453 592 37 kg

Ounces and Quarts to Liters

1 oz = 0.029 573 53 L
1 qt = 0.9463 L

Gallons to Liters

1 gal = 3.785 411 784 L

Fahrenheit to Celsius (Centigrade)

$°C = °F - 32 \times \frac{5}{9}$

°F	°C
-30	-34.45
-20	-28.89
-10	-23.34
-5	-20.56
0	-17.78
10	-12.22
20	-6.67
30	-1.11
32 (freezing)	0.00
40	4.44
50	10.00
60	15.56
70	21.11
80	26.67
90	32.22
100	37.78
212 (boiling)	100

Have a home gardening, decorating, or improvement project?
Look for these and other fine Creative Homeowner books wherever books are sold

1001 IDEAS FOR BETTER GARDENING
Tips on gardening methods and selecting plants for your landscape.

Over 450 photographs and illustrations.
256 pp.
8½" × 10⅞"
$24.95 (US)
$27.95 (CAN)
BOOK #: 274183

COMPLETE HOUSEPLANTS
Secrets to growing the most popular types of houseplants.

Over 480 photographs and illustrations.
224 pp.
9" × 10"
$19.95 (US)
$21.95 (CAN)
BOOK #: 274820

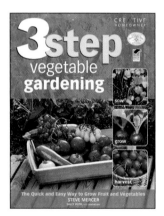

3 STEP VEGETABLE GARDENING
A quick and easy guide for growing your own fruit and vegetables.

Over 300 photographs.
224 pp.
8½" × 10⅞"
$19.95 (US)
$21.95 (CAN)
BOOK #: 274557

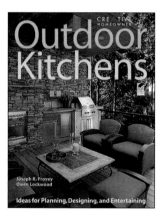

OUTDOOR KITCHENS
Planning and design advice from top professionals.

Over 335 photographs and illustrations.
224 pp.
8½" × 10⅞"
$21.95 (US)
$25.95 (CAN)
BOOK #: 277571

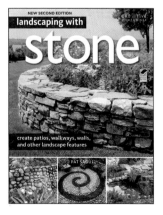

LANDSCAPING WITH STONE
Ideas for incorporating stone into the landscape.

Over 335 photographs.
224 pp.
8½" × 10⅞"
$19.95 (US)
$21.95 (CAN)
BOOK #: 274179

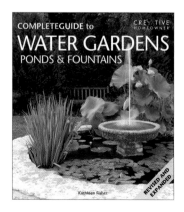

COMPLETE GUIDE TO WATER GARDENS, PONDS & FOUNTAINS
Secrets to creating garden water features.

Over 600 photographs and illustrations.
240 pp.
9" × 10"
$19.95 (US)
$21.95 (CAN)
BOOK #: 274458

For more information and to order direct, go to **www.creativehomeowner.com**